CLAREMONT BOY

CLAREMONT BOY

*My New Hampshire Roots
and the Gift of Memory*

℘

Joseph D. Steinfield

Dear Andrew
We have "Claremont" in common,
and much more. I send you my
best wishes,

Joe Steinfield
8/5/16

Bauhan Publishing
Peterborough · New Hampshire
2014

ISBN 978-0-87233-173-0
Library of Congress Cataloging-in-Publication Data

Steinfield, Joseph D., 1939-
  Claremont boy : my New Hampshire roots and the gift of memory /
Joseph D Steinfield.
    pages cm
  Includes bibliographical references and index.
  ISBN 978-0-87233-173-0 (alk. paper)
  1.   Claremont (N.H.)--Social life and customs--20th century--
Anecdotes. 2. New England--Social life and customs--20th century--
Anecdotes. 3. Steinfield, Joseph D., 1939---Homes and haunts. I. Title.
  F44.C65S75 2014
  974.2'75--dc23
                    2014011042

BAUHAN
PUBLISHINGLLC
PO BOX 117 PETERBOROUGH NEW HAMPSHIRE 03458
603-567-4430
WWW.BAUHANPUBLISHING.COM

Frontispiece: *Bar Mitzvah* Day, March 1, 1952

Joe Steinfield can be reached at JSteinfield@princelobel.com

Printed in the United States of America

For my children, Frank, Ken, and Liz,
and my grandchildren, Jacob, Susie, and Solomon.
I wrote these for you.

The memory of the righteous is a blessing

Proverbs 10:17

Contents

Foreword   10

Acknowledgements   12

FAMILY

My Grandmother and a Song From the Past   16

My Grandfather and the Gift of Love   19

My Grandfathers' Cemeteries and the Light That Never Goes Out   21

My Cousin Romaine and a Letter From the Old Country   25

My Cousin Chaim and a Story for Thanksgiving   28

My Refugee Cousin and the Tailor's Son   30

My First Name and the Mayor's Son   32

My Father's Day Memories and a Debt That Can't Be Repaid   34

My Father's Advice and Mr. Dean   36

My Father's Mill and Making Decisions   38

My Marx Brothers Cousins and Ellery Queen   41

My Father's Father and the Surname That Changed   43

My Father's Votes and My Mother's Apostasy   45

My Vertical Challenge and Passing the Beans   47

My Mother's Hobby and Roosevelt Grier   49

My Ski Trips and a Very Good Sport   51

My Mother's Decline and Words That Live On   53

My Uncle Eddie and the Right to Brag   56

My Uncle Bill and Counting Points   59

My In-Laws and Healing Old Wounds   61

My Bee Stings and the Tree Out Front   63

My Special Holiday and Perfect Grandchildren   65

My Daughter's Disclosure and Coming to Terms   67

My Unreserved Table and the Balloon Man   69

PEOPLE

My Partner Reg and Returning to Alabama   74

My Lost Plane and Daniel Ellsberg   76

My Blind Friend and Crossing the Street   78

My Birthmate and the Phenomenon of Email   80

My Friend Luis and the Extended Warranty   82

My Partner Dave and a House in Jaffrey   84

Our Neighbor and the End of an Era   86

My Neighbor Malcolm and the Naming of Houses   88

My Jaffrey Neighbor and the Last Flight   90

My Dearie Friend and a Life Fully Lived   92

My Summer Movies and Julia Child's Friend   94

My Friend Dick and the Epidemic of Man-Made Disasters   96

My Supreme Court Count and Justice Souter   98

My Friend's Son and Flag Burning   100

My Commute and the Gift of Life   102

My Elevator Ride and Valentine's Day Hearts   104

My Freshman Year and the Unorthodox Roommate   106

My Daughter-in-Law's Relative and the Boston Christmas Tree   109

My Hero Victor and Promises to His Mother   112

SPORTS

My Lifelong Addiction and Words to Live By   118

My Spring Fancy and a Lasting Disappointment   120

My Hot Corner and the Loss of Innocence   122

My High School Sports and the Last Basket   124

My Cousin's Bar Mitzvah and Dominic DiMaggio   126

My Visit to Fenway and a Tip of the Hat   128

My Favorite Sport and the Passage of Time   131

ARTS

My Teenage Jazz Festival and Duke Ellington   136

My Rock Star and Ozzy Osbourne's Conditions   139

My Love of Theatre and the Play I Missed   141

My Advice for Valentine's Day and the Limits of Social Media   144

My Favorite Poet and the Changing Seasons   146

My Red Record and an Overdue Apology   148

TRAVELS

My Missing Wallet and the Man at the Front Desk   152

My First Trip to Russia and the News Back Home   154

My Night at the Opera and the Duty Free Shop   156

My Visa Application and Testing for HIV   159

My Muslim Friend and the Jews of Maykop   162

My Trip to Washington and Holiday Greetings 165

My Russian Visa and the Announcement at Baggage Claim 168

My Icelandic Connection and a Run of Bad Luck 170

My Caribbean Cruise and Arriving Late for New Year's 172

My Left-Behind Snore Guard and Beating a Bum Rap 174

My Delayed Flight and Taco Bell 176

My Atlanta Visit and the Kindness of Strangers 178

My Trip to Rosebud and Languages That Won't Die 180

CLAREMONT

My Sister's Room and Memories of Christmas 184

My Fifth Grade Teacher and Valentine's Day 186

My Claremont Youth and the Things We Didn't Have 188

My Automobile Memories and the General Motors Bankruptcy 190

My Claremont Optimism and the Bankruptcy of Cities 192

My Life as a Salesman and the Radio That Never Arrived 194

My Hometown Newspaper and a Life Cut Short 196

My Facts and the Right to be Wrong 198

My High School's Songs and a Gift in Memory 200

"My Counselor" and the New Hampshire Impeachment 202

My Favorite Lawyer and Homeschooled Children 204

My High School Band and a Lesson in Politics 206

My High School Newsletter and Carrying the Torch 209

My Senior Year and the Most Important Teacher 211

My College Applications and the Dreaded Thin Envelope 213

My Latest Reunion and Where to Stay Next Time 215

My Small World and a Trip to the Past 217

My House at Edgewood and the Second Lightning Strike 220

My First Job and the Question of Identity 222

My One-Telegram Relatives and a Hero of Argentina 224

My Unwritten Book and The Jews of Claremont 227

Foreword

"My Unwritten Book and the Jews of Claremont," the last piece in this book, recalls a conversation many years ago with a man who had recently moved to New Hampshire. When I told him "I'm from Claremont," he asked what it had been like to grow up Jewish in a small New Hampshire town. I told him about my father and his immigrant parents, who moved there from Chelsea, Massachusetts, at the beginning of the twentieth century; and about my mother and her parents, also immigrants, who migrated from Boston to Littleton and Berlin, New Hampshire, before arriving in Claremont around 1930. He suggested I write a book and call it *The Jews of Claremont*.

That conversation of more than twenty years ago lingered in the back of my mind, but I didn't do anything about it. Instead, like so many things, my life as an essayist began by accident. In 2006, I attended a conference in California. One of the speakers was Daniel Ellsberg, who spoke about the act for which he became famous—his decision in 1971 to leak the Pentagon Papers to *The New York Times*. I went up to him and introduced myself. "Dan," I said, "I have a story to tell you."

On the plane back to Boston, I wrote "My Lost Plane and Daniel Ellsberg." By that time, my wife and I had been part-time residents of Jaffrey, New Hampshire, for twenty years, so it seemed appropriate to submit this "one shot" article to the *Monadnock Ledger-Transcript* in Peterborough.

The problem, I found, is that writing one remembrance is like eating one peanut. It just isn't enough. So I wrote another one, "My Cousin's *Bar Mitzvah* and Dominic DiMaggio." Although I didn't know it at the time, being Jewish and loving baseball would be recurring themes as I settled into writing a column every month. I would sometimes worry that I would run out of stories to tell, bringing my writing career to an untimely end. A new version of the classic anxiety dream, I suppose. Fortunately, something would then come to mind, or an event or newspaper story would trigger a memory, and I would write it down immediately, saved for at least another month.

What began as a diversion turned into my avocation, and I decided to call my column "Looking Back." The memories I have written about over the last several years are collected here, edited slightly to set them into the context of a memoir.

As a boy, I thought Claremont was the center of the universe. On a trip to New York City when I was five, I informed my mother and grandmother that we had a building higher than the Empire State Building. I don't know whether I remember saying that or whether I'm remembering that they told me about it later, but whatever the case, it came back to me many decades later in "My Facts and the Right to be Wrong."

I once heard that when a person from the North meets someone, he says, "What do you do?" A person from the South asks a different question, "Where are y'all from?" or "Where's your daddy from?" I prefer the southern version. My children and my friends know very well where I'm from, and naming this book *Claremont Boy* feels just right.

Like all trial lawyers, I tell stories for a living, but those are other people's stories. These are mine, a partial memoir told two or three pages at a time.

Joe Steinfield
April 2014

Acknowledgements

In April, 2006, my first article appeared in the Monadnock *Ledger-Transcript*'s "Moose" supplement. So it is fitting that I begin by thanking Jane Eklund, who indulged me by agreeing to publish the piece. I owe thanks as well to her successors as my *Ledger-Transcript* editors, Dave Anderson, Dave Solomon, Nick Reid, and Steve Leone.

My wife, Virginia Eskin, who appears in these pages as the "Pianist," has been incredibly helpful. She first visited Claremont not long after meeting me in 1984, and she has returned many times. It was her idea that I write about my Claremont years, and she has been my full partner in this endeavor.

My children, Frank, Ken, and Liz, have been a constant support. Almost from the outset, I have sent them drafts of the articles, and they have made countless improvements. Ken, in particular, has found grammatical and factual mistakes that eluded me, and I am grateful to all three of them. Thanks also go to my sister, Phyllis Foster, who clarified and corrected many of my faulty memories and provided many of the family photographs.

I owe an unpayable debt to those relatives and friends who appear and re-appear in these pages, especially my grandparents and parents. My mother's parents, Maurice and Lillian Firestone, lived in Claremont and were with me from my birth to adulthood. They helped me in ways unique to grandparents.

My father's family moved to Claremont around 1900. I never knew my father's father, for whom I am named. He died in 1911. And my grandmother, Bertha Steinfield, who survived my grandfather by more than three decades, died when I was very young. Even so, they are part of who I am.

My partners at Prince Lobel have given me the latitude of writing many of these pieces on company time, for which I am most grateful. And I thank those who have read these pieces and made helpful suggestions.

I wish to thank my friends and neighbors in Jaffrey, New Hampshire, and the people in neighboring towns who have sent emails, written letters, or stopped me on the street to tell me they enjoy what I write. One woman told me that she likes my stories because "you write about experiences we have all had." I can imagine no higher compliment.

Mary Ann Faughnan is a first-rate editor, and she made countless improvements to the manuscript. Nerissa Osborne has provided encouragement, energy, and expertise in helping market the book. Henry James created the wonderful cover, which captures the Claremont of my youth, and oversaw all of the graphics with the help of Brianna Morrissey. Kirsty Anderson took my rough pages and laid them out in a handsome book design. Finally, special thanks to Sarah Bauhan, my publisher, who responded with enthusiasm when I approached her with the idea of turning these pieces into a book.

My grandparents and my mother, c. 1913

Family

My Grandmother and a Song From the Past

My maternal grandmother came to this country from Dereczyn, Poland, in 1904. At Ellis Island she gave her name, Lillian Gerson (Gershuni). She soon made her way to Lowell, Massachusetts, where she lived with her cousin Eva Berlin. My grandmother took her cousin's name and became "Lily *Berlin.*"

My grandmother's mother, Chana

She met my grandfather, Maurice D. Firestone, and they moved to Boston and then to Littleton, New Hampshire, where they had a store. Like a lot of grandmothers, she was remarkable. She never learned to drive, but some things she just knew—how to cook, how to sew, how to judge quality.

During the 1920s, the violinist Jascha Heifetz, already famous, came to her home for Sunday dinners. I'm told that Heifetz suffered from hay fever, and came to New Hampshire for cleaner air, not to play the violin. Maybe he was also looking for good food. Somehow he heard about Mrs. Firestone's skill in the kitchen and became a frequent visitor.

My grandmother had another skill. She had a sweet voice, gentle and melodic. She knew Yiddish songs, and English ones too. One in particular she sang to me as a child, but as an adult I could only remember a few words, something about a "rainy afternoon" and ending with the word, "Good-bye." It was too late to ask my grandmother the name of the song, but the melody lingered in my ears, just as the aroma of her apple cake did in my nostrils. I've wondered whether she made that apple cake for the great Heifetz.

My grandmother, Lillian Firestone

Long after my grandmother died, I met a concert pianist named Virginia Eskin, who eventually became my second wife. My mother would tell her about living in Littleton, and I would tell her about growing up in Claremont. I told her that my grandmother could cook better than anybody, and sing too.

The Pianist is a collector, I am not. She started to buy old sheet music and give it to me so that I would have a collection of something. One day, she brought home a piece of music with a picture on the front of a man under an umbrella in pouring rain. I looked inside and found, at long last, the song from my childhood, "Call Me Up Some Rainy Afternoon." It is a wonderful song, with the kind of lyrics you don't find in music anymore:

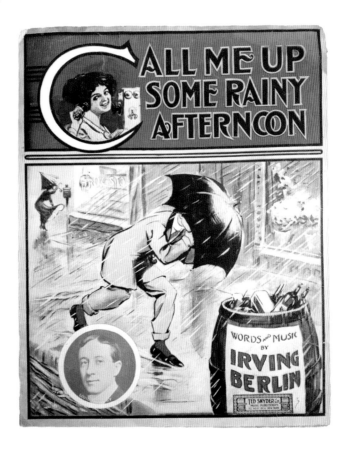

Think of all the joy and bliss,
We can hug and we can talk about the weather,
We can have a quiet little talk,
I will see that my mother takes a walk . . .

I'm sure it's just a coincidence, but the composer of the song I'd been looking for all those years turned out to be . . . Irving *Berlin.*

My Grandfather and the Gift of Love

My grandfather Firestone came to this country from Eastern Europe in 1904. He made his way from Poland to Liverpool, England, mostly by foot. With money his father gave him, he bought a ticket to America, steerage class. He never looked back.

He had no education, no money, and no English. He was, in other words, typical of thousands of immigrants who passed through Ellis Island at that time. He made his way to Boston, and later to New Hampshire—Littleton, Berlin, and finally Claremont. He learned English, but he never lost his accent.

He loved the Red Sox and saw Babe Ruth pitch at Fenway Park. Baseball helped Americanize him, and he passed his love of the sport on to me, as I have to my children and grandchildren. He spoke perfect baseball English. A lefthander was always a "southpaw," and a first-year player was always a "rookie."

He would drive me to Boston to see games—the Red Sox and, for a time, the Braves too. We talked about the players, Ted Williams especially. My grandfather was so proud of the fact that his son, my Uncle Eddie, a fighter pilot in World War II, had taught Ted how to fly. We went over the teams, eight in each league back then, and the batting averages of our favorite players. He would tell me about Babe Ruth and Walter Johnson, Ty Cobb and Tris Speaker.

He was completely self-educated, and his interests ranged far beyond baseball, especially to American history. He managed the Claremont office of the Metropolitan Life Insurance Company. After retiring at age sixty-five, he had time to read and to learn. He also had time to become a member of the New Hampshire legislature. He happily displayed a picture of himself standing next to Governor Lane Dwinell when an insurance bill he sponsored became law. How far he had come in half a century.

My mother was the oldest of his three children, each of whom had two children. Our grandfather adored his six grandchildren. And when a grandchild became engaged and brought his or her intended spouse

Maurice D. Firestone soon after his
arrival, c. 1906

to meet him, he told each of them, "Now you are my grandchild too."

From the time I learned to speak, he always asked the same question, "What did you do to earn your keep today?"

It was a good question, and I tried to give him a good answer. I can remember saying things like, "I ate my breakfast," or "I cleared my plate after dinner."

And I can remember his answer. "That's good."

When my mother offered me a quarter, or maybe it was a dime, for every "A" on my report card, he offered to match her for every time I *didn't* get an A. He never explained what he had in mind, but I think it was a message that grades aren't everything, and also a way of telling me that in his eyes, I was perfect.

We learned so much from him and his indomitable spirit. When he became gravely ill in 1970, I went to see him at the Mary Hitchcock Hospital in Hanover. He sent me away.

"I don't want you to remember me like this, but as I was," he told me.

I knew better than to argue. I did as he asked, with tears in my eyes, and I think of Maurice Firestone every day, as he was, with gratitude and love.

My Grandfathers' Cemeteries and the Light That Never Goes Out

I read an article some time ago about the Jews of Indonesia. I didn't know there were any, but since I was writing from time to time about the Jews of Claremont, the article naturally captured my interest. I learned that these Indonesian Jews, descended from early Dutch settlers, live in a place called Manado. Not surprisingly, there aren't many left.

The city recently built a sixty-two-foot-tall *menorah* (the candelabrum used in Jewish worship) on a nearby mountaintop. And there is a synagogue, the only one remaining in the country, but the nearest rabbi is in Singapore, so the Jews of Manado rely on "Rabbi Google" to learn about their ancestral faith. They barely have enough for a *minyan* (the quorum of ten adults necessary to conduct services), yet the eternal light burns over the holy ark as it does in every synagogue.

The part of the article that gnawed at me was mention of Manado's Jewish cemetery, overgrown with weeds and rarely visited. I decided it was time I visited the gravesites of my Steinfield grandparents. I remembered they were buried in West Roxbury, Massachusetts, but I didn't know the exact location, and there is nobody left to ask. So I did what the Manado Jews do—I consulted "Rabbi Google," and within minutes had the name of the cemetery, "*Adath Israel*" on Jeshuran Road. I also had the locations for my grandfather (back left row B #11) and my grandmother (front right row K #19). I remembered the last time I was there, for my Uncle Bill's funeral on my eighteenth birthday.

Finding Jeshuran Road was no simple task, but after asking several people for directions I came upon a group of cemeteries, all clustered together, neatly kept and weedless, one with the name "*Adas Yisroel.*" That seemed like the right place, so I set about looking for the designated locations. There are no lettered rows or numbered graves. I wandered around the "back left" and "front right," but I couldn't find my grandparents and finally gave up.

Not for long. I threw myself on the mercy of the Jewish Cemetery Association of Massachusetts, and a helpful woman said she would do

Front: Steinfield Grandparents, Bertha and Joseph (center and right)
Rear: My father (rear right) and his brothers Sam (middle) and Bill (left)

some research for me. That very day, she sent me a rudimentary map of *"Adas Yisroel,"* showing "back left" and "front right" and some letters, so off I went again, looking for my grandparents.

I found them. My grandmother Bertha's stone says "Beloved Mother Died October 21, 1943." My Uncle Bill, who never married, is to her right, her brother Max and her sister Ida and their spouses are to her left. Each has a separate gravestone in front of a large monument that says "Steinfield—Ruben—Marshall."

As I stood there I wondered, *Why isn't my grandfather there too?* Again, there was no one I could ask.

I then located my grandfather in "back left Row B." The large stone is inscribed, "In memory of our beloved father Joseph B. Steinfield Died Dec. 12, 1911, Age 44 years." Why "B?" His middle name was David, like mine. Well, I know they called him "Burt."

Back in the 1950s, the Jews of Claremont decided to have their own cemetery. My Grandfather Firestone organized that project so that, in his words, "we won't have to *schlep* (Yiddish for "lug") them to Boston." My father was the first to sign up, and he picked the plot nearest the entrance so that we wouldn't have a problem finding him. My mother is next to him. Whenever I go to Claremont, Meyer-David Cemetery is my first stop.

My latest stop, the resting place of my Steinfield grandparents whom they had to *schlep* from Claremont to Boston, is now burned in my memory. Before leaving the cemetery, following the Jewish tradition, I put stones on their graves. Later that day, I looked up "Jeshuran," the name of the road. It comes from the Old Testament and means "beloved."

Meyer-David Cemetery, Claremont

Family

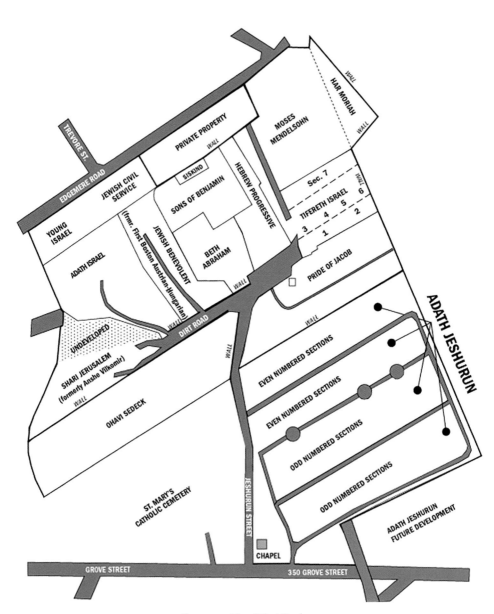

Cemetery Map, West Roxbury

My Cousin Romaine and a Letter From the Old Country

My mother's parents were born in the "Old Country," on dates long since forgotten. My grandmother's small village, Dereczyn, was Poland then, became part of Russia in 1939, and, if it still exists, is today part of the country called Belarus. When she lived there, it must have been a lot like "Anatevka," the fictional *shtetl* in Russia where life was as precarious as a *Fiddler on the Roof*.

My grandmother's uncle, Isaac Bernstein, also came from Dereczyn. I never met the man, but as a boy growing up in Claremont, I heard about this relative who left the Old Country in the late nineteenth century and became a successful businessman in Lowell, Massachusetts. I also heard about a trip he made, not long before the War.

In 1938, after forty-nine years in this country, Uncle Bernstein returned to Dereczyn because, in the words of a letter written after his visit "in the name of the families," he "yearned to see his native place" and to "embrace his sisters and relatives." I came across the letter among my mother's effects some years ago. It is undated, but it begins "A happy and prosperous new year to our brothers—Jews residing at Lowell, Mass., U.S. of America," which would place it around September 26th, the date of the Jewish New Year in 1938.

The letter refers to my grandmother, "Mrs. Fierstone (sic) residing at Claremont N.H." and says she was the granddaughter of Tamara Bernstein who, I assume, was Uncle Bernstein's mother. The letter also engages in some familial namedropping, pointing out that on her grandfather's side my grandmother was related to a famous rabbi, Isaac Elchanan Spector. I grew up hearing about this family member, said to be the wisest man in Lithuania in the nineteenth century.[1]

---

1 Rabbi Elchanan (1817–1896) served as Chief Rabbi of Kovno, the capital city of Lithuania. According to historian Gilbert Klapperman, his picture "hung on the wall of almost every Jewish home in Russia." An early supporter of Zionism, he advised Baron Rothschild that the way to deal with the biblical mandate to let the land lie fallow every seventh year, which threatened to undo years of agricultural progress in Palestine, was to sell the land, temporarily, to a gentile. See Shimoff, *Rabbi Isaac Elchanan Spektor*, pages 121–137 (New York: Yeshiva University Press, 1959). The

A HAPPY AND PROSPEROUS NEW-YEAR.
To our brothers-Jews residing at Lowell Mass, U. S. of America.

We wish a Happy New-Year, ful of joy and satisfaction to our brothers, residing at town Lowell Mass, and particularly to Mr. Isaac Bernstein with his children, by reason of the good deeds and favors done to us.

As a messenger of God appeared in our small town Dereczyn Mr. Isaac Bernstein. God Himself has evidently sent him to us to save in case of need tens of Jewish families.

You must be pround, Jews of Lowell-Mass, that amongst you such a man is living.

We, however, are proud, that amongst us he was born.

We, therefore, wish to tell you what Mr. Isaac Bernstein has done and we shall as well give a description of his earlier years and of his descent.

Isaac Bernstein comes out of a noble Jewish family. His high merits of heart and character he inherited from his parents, Eliash and Tamara.

His father, Eliash, was a wise man, possesing all the erudition of the Talmud. His sayings and aphorisms are still circulating amongst us till this day.

Mr. Isaac Bernstein inherited his kindness of heart, energy and enterprise from his mother, Tamara.

Tamara Bernstein comes out of a family, which has given famos Rabbies and writers. Her cousin was the Hebrew writer, Bershadzki, author of the book „Kneged Haserem" (Against the current) and her nephew is the Rabbi Sh Jogiel, known in whole Poland and Palestine. It is worthy of mentioning that Mrs. Fierstone, residing at Claremont N. H. is a granddaugther of Tamara Bernstein and from the side of her grandfather Giershuni she comes out of the famos Rabbi Isaac-Elchanan, whose name bears now the largest Rabinic Collegium at New-York

This is approximately the origin of Mr. Isaac Bernstein.

The townlet Dereczyn, the place of birth of Mr. Isaac Bernstein, is full of ruins of the castles, left by Earl Sapieha and is situated in a picturesque place abundant of wood and lakes. Impregnated with the freedom of nature the impetuos character of Young Mr. Isaac Bernstein couldn't bear the oppressing atmosphere of the small town fanatism and one morning the 17 years old Mr. Bernstein left his birth place turning himself to America. 49 years passed from that moment till now.

Much water flowed down the river Missisipi, and many changes were in the life of Mr. Isaac Bernstein and in the lives of American Jews. But we, living in this place of half-cultured, half-wild people, have lived through years of war, pogroms, hunger, pain and need.

After so many years Mr. Isaac Bernstein yearned to see his native place. He wished to see the moss-grown graves of his parents, wanted to embrace his sisters and relatives and so he didn't forget on us though his fate put him high over us.

He came to us has seen our suffering and destitution and with a broad hand he began to apply help and money to his sisters, relatives and filantropical institutions. Mr. Isaac Bernstein said: I want to wipe out the tears from your eyes. He helped out 25 families, who improved their existence and indirectly helped another 25 families.

Dear Mr. Isaac Bernstein: Let grow your feeling of self-respect, and let it be fct you the greatest satisfaction, that you put on their feet tens of Jewish families that their families are not crying for a piece of bread. With blessings in our mouths we pronounce the name „Isaac Bernstein" who blew into our dry bones the spirit of life and into our pain-struck hearts the spirit of courage that our brother cf America didn't forget on us.

We wish you, Mr. Isaac Bernstein for your kind deeds, to live to happiness, satisfaction and joy together with your children: Bannet, Georges and Ella with their families. We shall remember you for ever our children and grandchildren will remember you as well.

Bo proud, Jews of Lowell-Mass, that amongst you is living such a great man.

In name of the families:

M. Feldman, Ch. Feldman, H. Dworecki, L. Winiacki, E. Blum (Warszawa), Ch. Wajsztejn, Sz. Stukalski, L. Stukalski, J. Stukalski, A. Nadel, M. Bernstein, R. Pud, S. Iwieniecka, Sz. Szymielewicz, G. Harkawy, J. Benjaminowicz (Jerusalem), Sz. Tejtel (Warszawa), H. Fridman (Białystok), Z. Borowski (Augustow), H. Czarny (Nowogródek), A. Pud (Grodno).

In name of the institutions:

„Bikur Cholim", „Linath Cedek", „G.-Ch. Kase", „Frauen-Ferein", „Keren-Kajemeth", „Keren-Hajesod", „Bet-Jawne", „Bet-medrasz Jaszan", „Bet-medrasz Ec", „Bet-Hakneseth", „Waad Hakhila" Dereczyn.

Written by **Girsz Feldman**
Lida (Poland) 17 Kwietnia Nr. 4.

Ruchele in Poland, 1938

But this story is not about that side of the family. It is about Uncle Bernstein, and the great *mitzvah* (act of human kindness) that he performed. He may have been homesick, but he had other reasons for taking his trip. The letter says that he came "to wipe out the tears from our eyes." The letter goes on to say that he "blew into our dry bones the spirit of life and into our painstruck hearts the spirit of courage that our brother of American didn't forget on us."

Uncle Bernstein brought clothes and money. When it came time for him to leave, with tears in his eyes, Uncle Bernstein asked whether there was anything else he could do.

His sister, Pesha, said, "Yes, there is. Take Ruchele," pointing to her teenage daughter.

The letter does not mention Ruchele, much less explain how Uncle Bernstein, a widower nearing age seventy, managed to carry out this act of charity and love. I will leave that part of the story to your imagination.

She became my Cousin Romaine. "Ruchele" should have been "Rachel," but my mother knew an elegant Boston woman whose name was "Romaine," and she thought that name better suited her newly arrived cousin. Romaine married a wonderful man named Irving Efros, lived elegantly on Central Park West in New York, and died in her eighties after a long and useful life.

Rabbi Isaac Elchanan Theological Seminary, part of Yeshiva University in New York, is named after him.

My Cousin Chaim and a Story for Thanksgiving

There comes a time in life when people start reading obituaries. For me, that began several years ago, and it continues to this day. I've met some pretty interesting people. Too bad I was late.

I recently read about the life of Norman Katz and wished I had known him. Mr. Katz spent three of his 88 years with his father and aunt in the woods of Lithuania, hiding from the Nazis. In 1951 he came to the United States, where he found freedom and opportunity.

Our family had its own version of Norman Katz, my Cousin Chaim Feldman. Like my grandmother Firestone, he was from Dereczyn, Poland. As the Nazis approached their village in 1943, he took his wife Lisa, and their sons Martin and Stephen, into the forest. Martin was seven years old, Stephen was four. They moved continuously, mostly at night, and during much of that time Chaim carried his younger son on his back. Fortunately, he was a bear of a man.

Like Mr. Katz, they survived the Holocaust. In 1947, they arrived in Claremont, where my cousins entered Bluff School without a word of English and lived with my grandparents for a year. Chaim and Lisa went to New York, where his sister Romaine lived. The boys grew up in the Bronx, attended City College, married, and had children.

Front: Martin, Stephen, me
Rear: Chaim, my father, my grandfather 1947

In the late 1970s, NBC broadcast a four-part mini-series called *The Holocaust*. A few months later, I attended the *bar mitzvah* of my Cousin Martin's son. After the ceremony we gathered at Martin's home, located in one of New York City's nicest suburbs. We stood around the swimming pool, while the catering staff passed hors d'oeuvres.

Cousin Chaim came over to me. "So, Choi (Joey)," he asked in his heavily accented English, "Did ya see *The Holocaust*?"

"Yes, Cousin Chaim," I replied.

He looked at me. "Vat did ya tink?"

"It was horrible," I answered.

"I vant ya t' imagine someting a tousand times verse."

"I don't think I can do that," I said.

"Vell, it's OK, Choi," he replied, "because ya still vouldn't know how terrble it vas."

The movie *Schindler's List* came out in 1993. Martin called and asked if I had seen it. I hadn't. "My father was my Schindler," he said. I saw the movie that night.

Lisa died first. At Chaim's funeral, the young rabbi regretted that he hadn't known my cousin but said he would do his best to convey a sense of the man, based on his conversations with Martin, Stephen, and Romaine.

The rabbi began by observing that this man had led a quiet life, content to raise his family and count his blessings. In every person's life, the rabbi went on, there comes a time when you are called upon to do something important. For Chaim, that time was 1943, and he was called upon to save his family. As the rabbi described those two years in the woods, I looked at the backs of two heads, Martin's and Stephen's, and wondered, "What must they be remembering?" The question answered itself.

"One person of integrity can make a difference," according to the well-known writer and Holocaust survivor Elie Wiesel. Mr. Katz surely did, to his wife, his children, his grandchildren, and to all who knew him. The same is true of my Cousin Chaim. I think of him often and wish I had known him better.

My Refugee Cousin and the Tailor's Son

In the Claremont of my youth, nearly everyone's grandparents were immigrants. Some were from French-speaking Canada, some were from Scotland, Ireland, or Italy, and others were from Eastern Europe. My grandparents were among that latter group, as was Mr. Gelfand, who had a tailor shop on Pleasant Street, one flight up.

He was a small man, like most members of his generation whom I knew, and he spoke with an accent. I used to see him when I went downtown after school, since his shop was over the Pleasant Sweet Restaurant, where we went for ice cream or a soda. He always greeted me, asked me how I was doing, and made me feel like a special person.

I have a soft spot for Mr. Gelfand for another reason. Although my mother took care of me when I got sick, it was he who rescued me in a *real* emergency, when I accidentally ripped my pants one day in the middle of town. Not just any rip, mind you, but a very serious and embarrassing event in my young life.

It was around the time I tore my pants that my cousins Martin and Stephen arrived. It was 1947, and they had survived the war by hiding in the forest. A few years after the war ended, they and their parents made it to my grandparents' home in Claremont. By the end of the year they were at grade level, learning to play sports (no time or opportunity for that hiding in the forest or in the displaced persons camp), and feeling like Americans.

That spring, they left New Hampshire for New York, where their parents had opened a small neighborhood store. The boys continued in school and eventually became CPAs, shedding their accents along the way.

My cousin Martin found a job in a firm that prospered greatly over the years, specializing in financial services for the music, motion picture, and television industries. They had offices in several cities, and clients whose names we all know. Martin soon became a partner, and went to London for a few years to manage the firm's newest office. And his name became part of the firm's name, which began with "Gelfand," the senior member of the firm. Yes, my cousin had joined the son of the Claremont tailor, Mr. Gelfand.

An architect friend of mine designed the New York apartment of the singer Carly Simon. My friend asked Ms. Simon whether she could recommend an accountant. "Yes," Ms. Simon told her, "You should see Marshall Gelfand. His firm is called Gelfand, Rennert & Feldman. They specialize in representing entertainers, but I'm sure he would be glad to help you." My friend made an appointment, and went to see Mr. Gelfand. "You know," she said, "I'm pretty good at accents. You sound like you're from New Hampshire."

"You're right," he replied.

"You wouldn't by any chance happen to be from Claremont?" my friend asked.

"That's exactly where I am from," Mr. Gelfand said.

"I know someone from Claremont," said my friend, giving him my name and asking if he knew me.

"Of course I do," he told my friend. "I'm a good deal older, but our families knew each other very well."

Mr. Gelfand said that he was spending a lot of time in the firm's California office and wanted to introduce her to one of his partners. That was fine with her, so he picked up the phone and asked his partner, Martin Feldman, if he could join them. The three of them then talked for a few minutes, and my friend said she would be pleased to have Mr. Feldman as her accountant.

"I'm sure you will enjoy working with him," said Mr. Gelfand. "He and I have been together for a long time, and you can't do better. By the way, Marty is Joe Steinfield's cousin."

What he did not tell her was the rest of the story, that my cousin Martin survived the Holocaust by hiding in the forest with his family for two years and spent his first year in this country living with my grandparents on Myrtle Street in Claremont.

Today, Martin is retired, comfortable, and living in suburban New York City. When I go to Claremont, and run into people who were there in the 1940s, they sometimes ask, "How are the refugees?"

My First Name and the Mayor's Son

When I was a kid growing up in Claremont, they called me "Joey." Hardly anyone does that now, or "Joseph" either. My name is "Joe," and that suits me fine. Still, "Joey" has a nostalgic ring, reviving memories of friends and relatives, including my aunt in Albany, New York, who called me by that name.

In my essay entitled "My Cousin Romaine and a Letter from the Old Country," I wrote about my grandmother's Uncle Bernstein, who went back to Poland in 1938, on the eve of the Holocaust, and rescued his sister's teenage daughter. He was a widower in his seventies, and I left it to the reader's imagination, as I do once again, to figure out how he managed to obtain travel papers so she could come to America. She became my cousin Romaine, lived a long life, and performed many *mitzvot*—the Yiddish word for good deeds.

One of those deeds began in the late 1960s. This was at the beginning of the time known as *Détente*, when relations between the United States and Russia started to thaw. With her husband, Irving, Romaine made the first of several trips from their home on Central Park West to Russia, taking suitcases filled with clothes, household goods, and gifts for Irving's relatives—his sister, a government scientist, and her grown son and his family.

Irving's relatives lived in an obscure city in the Ural Mountains, a place that Americans did not visit. Clearing customs in Moscow and then traveling by train to this distant city with all those suitcases posed major obstacles.

A man named Erastus Corning III, a native of Albany, New York, and the son of its mayor, was in charge of the Pan American Airlines Moscow office. Fluent in Russian and accustomed to dealing with the bureaucracy, Erastus met Romaine and Irving when they first arrived at Sheremetyevo Airport, and he helped them cut through the red tape. Over the course of several visits, my cousin Romaine and Irving became very close to Erastus and his second wife, treating them as the children they never had. Erastus told Romaine that he was from Albany, and

My elegant cousin Romaine

Romaine told Erastus she had a cousin who lived there.

Meanwhile, back at that time, an interesting lawsuit was unfolding in probate court in Cambridge, Massachusetts. The issue before the court was whether two young children should live with their mother in the United States, or with their father, an American living in Moscow with his second wife.

One day, shortly after returning from one of her trips to Russia, Romaine called her cousin, my Aunt Myrtle, the one who lived in Albany, New York.

Romaine poured her heart out. "This wonderful man, your mayor's son, has a terrible problem, and I'm so worried. He's in the middle of a custody lawsuit, and I don't know if he has a good lawyer."

My aunt reassured our mutual cousin. "Don't worry, Romaine. It's Joey."

My Father's Day Memories and a Debt That Can't Be Repaid

I hadn't intended to write a Father's Day column this year but decided to do so after reading an article in *The New York Times* called "Remembrances of My Father," by Charles M. Blow.

Mr. Blow wrote that when he was young his father was rarely around. He was too busy with wine and women, and when he was there he was still distant. He ignored his son, both emotionally and physically. He openly claimed fatherhood only one time, when he introduced his son to some of his cronies as "my boy," the last two words of the son's touching article.

My father and me, Lake Sunapee, 1942

I think about my own father every Father's Day, and on most other days as well. He died in 1957 at age sixty-six after being ill for many years with heart disease and high blood pressure. I remember when I was nine we went to Durham, North Carolina, to visit him for a week. He had gone there for treatment—the Duke University rice diet. I don't think the diet did him much good, but I checked online recently and see they are still offering that program.

Frank Steinfield, born in Chelsea, Massachusetts, in 1891, was conservative in politics and in life. His father, for whom I am named, brought the family to Claremont around 1900, the second Jewish family in the town, and my father lived there for the rest of his life. He and his two brothers owned the Claremont Waste Manufacturing Company. He was a member of the Elks Club, where he played poker weekly, a thirty-second degree Mason, an ardent fisherman, and a true believer in the Republican Party.

He was devoted to my mother. In his eyes, she could do no wrong. When he became a father, he was middle-aged, more than two-thirds through his life. He always looked at my older sister and me as if we were miracles he never expected.

When I was an adolescent and became impatient or sarcastic with my aging and ill father, my mother, whose name was Irene, would chastise me. My father would always intervene, "Now Renee, never mind, I understand him." And he surely did.

If one measures the quality of one's years on a happiness scale, my father wouldn't have scored very well, at least from what I can remember. Beyond his poor health, his life was deeply scarred by his relationship with his older brother. They were partners in their flock manufacturing business, but for reasons I have never discovered, they did not speak.

If, on the other hand, you look at quality of life in terms of a person's character and reputation, he would have earned a very high score. I know that partly from what I could see, even at a relatively young age, and very much from what people who knew him have told me. To this day I can hear my father saying that only one thing in life really counts—your good name.

Charles Blow's father left him very little, really, just those two words, "my boy." By comparison, my father left me a great deal. I've often wondered how I could acknowledge my debt to him, if not repay it. The best I've been able to come up with is to remember his wise counsel, his sense of right and wrong, and try to emulate his values as a father and as a person. And I did one other thing. I gave his name to my first child.

My Father's Advice and Mr. Dean

My father taught me how to drive on a standard-shift 1953 Chevy. "Just remember where the brake is," he told me. He was a better teacher than driver. His fender-benders were known throughout Sullivan County.

Around 1918, after the United States became involved in the Great War (now known as World War I), he and his two brothers were operating their factory, but apparently they also had another business, a partnership in Claremont called "B. Steinfield's Sons." I think they were in the scrap metal business, which, as the name suggests, was their father's business.

My father always told me it was a great business but that I should become a lawyer. That way, he said, "Anytime you feel like it, you can close the door and go fishin'." I've always thought that was an interesting way to look at the profession I eventually entered.

Starting this month, I'm taking his advice and closing the door on Wednesday afternoons to do something else—not to go "fishin'" but to teach a course at University of New Hampshire Law School in Concord. The other day, just out of curiosity, I checked to see whether my father was ever involved in any New Hampshire lawsuits.

Sure enough, he was. And, wouldn't you know, it had to do with an automobile accident. According to the official New Hampshire Supreme Court Reports for 1920, an unidentified "partner" of B. Steinfield's Sons failed to apply the brake soon enough and ran into a man named Dean. Mr. Dean sued, and the partnership paid the amount awarded by the court.

My father asked his automobile insurer, the Massachusetts Bonding and Insurance Company, to reimburse him for the amount paid, but the company refused to do so. He wasn't about to take no for an answer, so he filed a lawsuit on the theory that he was a partner in "B. Steinfield's Sons" and as such was personally responsible for the partnership's debts. The court agreed, referring to the driver in its opinion as "the one who was driving the machine."

There's more to the story. The insurance company still didn't want to pay and claimed my father should have filed the suit within ninety days, as required by the insurance policy, and not waited four months after the partnership paid Mr. Dean. This produced an entirely separate opinion in the New Hampshire Supreme Court Reports for 1921. My father won again, this time under a 1918 federal law called the "Soldiers' and Sailors' Relief Act." My father was in the Army during most of the four months, and that period of time, the Court ruled, didn't count.

My father never told me about this case, or about the time my grandmother Bertha took on Monadnock Mills for flooding her property—and won! You can read about that case in the 1923 Reports.

As for Mr. Dean, the Court doesn't identify which of "B. Steinfield's Sons" drove the "machine" that hit him. I think I know.

Sullivan,
May 4, 1920.

FRANK STEINFIELD *v.* MASSACHUSETTS BONDING AND INSURANCE CO.

An insurer against the liability imposed on another by law "by reason of the ownership, maintenance and use" of an automobile is liable for the amount chargeable to the plaintiff on account of a judgment, recovered against the firm of which he is a member, for injury received by a third person from the operation of the car by a co-partner about the partnership's business.

ASSUMPSIT, on an indemnity policy. The defendants insured the plaintiff against liability for loss imposed on him by law "by reason of the ownership, maintenance and use" of his automobile. The plaintiff was a partner in the firm of B. Steinfield Sons and used the machine in the partnership business.

One of the partners while driving the machine, ran into one Dean, and he recovered a judgment against the firm, which the firm satisfied, and a deduction was made from the interest of the plaintiff in the partnership business. The question whether the plaintiff can maintain this action was transferred from the May term, 1919, of the superior court by *Marble*, J., without a ruling.

Hurd & Kinney (Mr. Hurd orally), for the plaintiff.

Streeter, Demond, Woodworth & Sulloway (Mr. Jonathan Piper orally), for the defendants.

YOUNG, J. If the language of the policy is given its ordinary meaning, the defendants are liable for any loss the plaintiff sustains

My Father's Mill and Making Decisions

My father and his older brother started a business called the Claremont Waste Manufacturing Company. I remember thinking as a kid, "What an odd thing to do, to make waste." The plant was on the Sugar River, and people in town called it the "shoddy mill." I never knew what that meant, but I recently looked it up and learned that "shoddy" is a term for waste from loosely woven fabrics. So I guess the company's nickname made some sense.

They made flock, which is hard to define but you know it when you see it. It's the fuzzy stuff on greeting cards, or wallpaper, a sort of imitation velvet. Not the world's most important product, but they knew a man who had a machine that could produce it from rags. My father told me that at one time the company did one hundred percent of the world's flock business, which is pretty good when you think about it.

My father's work life was interrupted by World War I, although he never got farther than North Carolina. He came back to the town and the mill and eventually met my mother, whose family had moved down from Berlin. The business did well enough that my mother had a new car every two years, which used to be the way. My father could probably have done the same, but he drove a Chevy or a used car until it wouldn't run anymore. He was not the least bit materialistic.

He did have one indulgence—his family—perhaps due to the fact that he didn't marry until age forty and became a father when other men his age were becoming grandfathers. He also had a great sadness—his relationship with Sam, his brother and business partner.

After years of not speaking, the brothers finally agreed that they would end their unhappy partnership—one would sell his half of the company to the other. My father, in failing health with heart disease, asked if I would like him to buy the business. "I'm only sixteen," I reminded him. He offered to hire someone to run the company until I grew up.

"Sell it," I said. And he did.

My father had an excellent lawyer from Concord and, for the last two days of negotiations, a prominent Boston lawyer as well. When the Boston lawyer's bill came, I thought my father would have a heart attack on the spot. He showed it to me—"For Services Rendered" followed by a hefty number. He asked what I thought.

"I think you should pay it," I said. And he did.

About fifteen years later, I was a lawyer myself and had a case for a schoolteacher that got some attention in the newspapers. The *Boston Herald* reporter, if you can believe it, was from Claremont.

One day the telephone rang, and it was the Boston lawyer who had helped my father. He told me he had read about my teacher case, his son was a teacher with a similar problem, and he would like to consult with me. I told him that I knew who he was, and I reminded him that he had helped my father many years before. I didn't mention his bill or my father's reaction to it.

He remembered the matter very well, we reminisced a bit, and then we talked about his son's situation. After an hour or so on the phone, he thanked me and told me to be sure and send him a bill.

I never did.[2]

Paperweight with mirror on back

---

2 When my uncle, Sam Steinfield, was buying his cemetery plot, he asked "Where's Frank going to be?" Told that my father had purchased the plot nearest the entrance, he said, "I may as well be next to him." So the two brothers, divided in life, were united in death.

Family

My father as a young man

Letterhead

My Marx Brothers Cousins and Ellery Queen

Groucho, Harpo, Chico, and Zeppo were not my relatives, but my father's cousins, the four Miller Brothers, were. People in Claremont used to call them "the Marx Brothers," so the title of this piece isn't exactly a lie, it's more like an exaggeration.

Somehow the Miller family found their way from the Old Country to Claremont, probably due to the fact that the Steinfields were already there, and Dora Miller and my grandmother Bertha were sisters, and their husbands Hirsch ("Harry") and my grandfather Joseph ("Burt") may have been cousins. I'm not sure just when Hirsch and Dora, their four sons and one daughter (Goldie) arrived from Russia, but Claremont town records show that the sixth Miller child, Ida, was born there in the spring of 1907. There was one child yet to come, Bess ("Betty"), born in Claremont in 1909. She plays an important role in this story.

I have a clear memory of the Miller brothers, Burt, Hy, Ben, and Dave. We saw them quite often, either at Lake Sunapee or in Claremont when they would come to Stevens High School reunions. They would show up, and everyone would start laughing. I don't have as clear a memory of the Miller sisters.

At one time, Ellery Queen was this country's most popular mystery writer. Between 1929 and 1971 "he" wrote over 30 novels, all featuring a detective named "Ellery Queen." Several of them are set in a town named "Wrightsville." I had never read any Ellery Queen mysteries until recently when, thanks to an article in Claremont's *Eagle Times*, I learned that "Wrightsville" is actually Claremont. So I sent away for *Double, Double,* a 1949 mystery novel that takes place in the not-so-fictional town of "Wrightsville." It's a terrific book, filled with murder, mayhem, and plot twists. And yes, Wrightsville is unmistakably Claremont, right down to the hotel on the square and the mills on lower Main Street. The book doesn't say so, but one of those mills was my father's factory.

Who was Ellery Queen? Actually, the question should be "Who *were* Ellery Queen?" because he was two people, neither of whom was named Ellery Queen. One was Frederick Dannay and the other was his cousin, Manfred ("Manny") Lee.

Manny Lee and Hy Miller, the funniest of the four brothers, met in college, and Hy introduced Manny to his kid sister Betty. They married in 1927. A year or two later, Manny teamed up with his cousin Fred, and somehow they came up with the name "Ellery Queen." By then Manny had visited Claremont several times, even though the Millers no longer lived there.

I remember hearing from my parents that one of our Miller relatives was married to Ellery Queen. Maybe they said "had been married," since Manny and my cousin Betty divorced before I was born. I think that means that I wasn't related to "Ellery Queen," at least by that marriage.

However, they had a daughter named Jacquelin. For a time she was married to my cousin Bob, and her last name became "Steinfield." So I guess Jacquelin is my "double, double" relative, once my second cousin by way of her mother (my father's cousin Betty), and once by way of her marriage to my cousin Bob.

Here's the mystery: When my two cousins were married, did I somehow become related to Manny Lee and, therefore, to Ellery Queen?

It's too complicated for me to figure out.[3]

---

3 Thanks to my cousin, Carl Steinfield (Bob was his brother), who sent me two articles from Claremont's *Eagle-Times* ("The Mysterious Ellery Queen," August 19, 2013, and "City Resembles Fake Town Created by Ellery Queen," August 27, 2013). I am also indebted to *Eagle-Times* correspondent Arthur Vidro, whose research provided many of the facts included in this piece.

My Father's Father and the Surname That Changed

"I wonder what'll become of MY name when I go in?
I shouldn't like to lose it at all . . ."

Lewis Carroll (1832–1898)
Through the Looking Glass, and What Alice Found There, 1871

If you Google my last name, the first thing that happens is the computer tells you you've made a mistake and shows "results for Steinfeld." All my life people have wanted to eliminate the second "i" from the name, and the Internet does the same thing. The first entry belongs to an actress named "Hailee Steinfeld," and with one mouse click you can eliminate the "t" and go straight to "Jerry Seinfeld."

If you persist, however, you can find the name spelled correctly, with the "t" and both "i"s. There's Charles, a college professor in Michigan; Arlene, a lawyer in Dallas; Paul, a doctor in Philadelphia; and quite a few others. I don't recognize any of them, and I don't know where they got my last name. So much for my childhood understanding that we were the only Steinfield family.

I was once asked to speak to a group of women psychiatrists on the subject of testifying in court as an expert witness. I accepted the invitation, arrived at the host's home, and gave my talk. Several hands went up, and a doctor asked me to comment about a particular case.

Given her professional expertise, she could no doubt tell that I had no idea what she was talking about. She explained that the case had been featured on the PBS program "Frontline" and told about a psychiatrist who served as an expert witness and, by the time the case was over, ended up getting sued. I said I hadn't seen the program and knew nothing about the case.

At that point the host, the doctor who had invited me, stood up and said, "Oh, my God, I invited the wrong Steinfield." It seems that the Colorado case involved a lawyer of the same name, or almost. I think his name was "Steinfeld" with one "i."

There are many stories about how immigrants to America acquired their names. You may have heard the one about the Jewish immigrant who arrives at Ellis Island and is so nervous that when the inspector asks his last name he says *"Sheyn fergessen"* (Yiddish for "I already forget"). The inspector writes his name on the form—"Sean Ferguson." There's another one about the tongue-tied immigrant who could only smile. The inspector wrote down "Smiley."

My father's father, for whom I am named, came to this country from Lithuania with his wife Bertha and their infant son in 1889 or 1890. They lived in Chelsea, Massachusetts, where my father, Frank, was born in 1891.

My father didn't tell me too much about his childhood, but I remember hearing about trips with his father by horse and wagon, peddling junk across Massachusetts and into New Hampshire. He also told me that in the Old Country the family's last name was "Pollak." When they arrived in this country, a relative met them at the boat and told my grandfather that "Pollak" wasn't an American enough name. "Take my name," he told my grandfather, and informed the customs official that these new arrivals were named "Steinfield" (with two "i"s). I always doubted that story.

A few years after the recently minted "Steinfields" moved to Claremont, the Miller family (Hirsch and my grandfather's sister, Dora) joined them. The youngest Miller child, Betty, is the cousin who married Ellery Queen. In my essay "My Marx Brothers Cousins and Ellery Queen," I wrote that Dora and my grandmother Bertha were sisters. In true Ellery Queen fashion, Betty's daughter, my cousin Jackie, recently cleared up a mystery I didn't know existed, which is how our families are related. She sent me a picture of her grandmother Miller and wrote, "Her maiden name was Dora Pollak, and she was an innkeeper's daughter."

This is what is known as an "aha moment," an instant of sudden comprehension. Our grandmothers weren't sisters at all. And my doubts were unfounded—our last name really *was* Pollak. My grandfather changed it, but *his sister*, Dora, never did, at least until she married Hirsch Miller.

My Father's Votes and My Mother's Apostasy

When my parents married, he was forty, she was twenty. As far as he was concerned, she was worth waiting for and could do no wrong.

It would be an understatement to say that my father was a Republican. He began voting in 1912, voted in twelve presidential elections, and never crossed over to the "D" column. Back then you could save time by putting an "X" in one box and vote the "straight Republican ticket."

First it was Taft in 1912, and last it was Eisenhower in 1956. In between, in ten presidential elections, he voted for Hughes, Harding, Coolidge, Hoover (twice), Landon, Wilkie, Dewey (also twice), and Eisenhower. My dad had a pretty good record in the 1920s, then went into a slump in the '30s and '40s, but emerged a winner his last two times at the ballot box.

How do I know this? He told me so in a conversation I initiated when I was around sixteen.

"Dad, you're a Republican, right?"

"Yes, I sure am," he replied.

"You have friends who are Democrats," I said.

"Of course," my father answered, without saying just how many or who they were.

I pressed on. "Would you ever vote for a Democrat?"

"Yes, I would," he said.

"Have you ever done so?" I asked him.

He paused, as if trying to remember, then said, "No, not that I can recall."

"Well, Dad, you've been voting since when, 1912?"

"That's right, I turned twenty-one that year," he told me.

I did a quick calculation. "So, you've voted in eleven elections and you've never voted for a Democrat. How do you explain that?"

Without hesitation my father answered my question: "Because there's never been a good Democrat."

The voters of New Hampshire didn't always see it that way. Twice they supported Woodrow Wilson, a Democrat, but then they got in line with my father and favored Republicans Harding, Coolidge, and Hoover. History hasn't treated those three too favorably, although I remember my father's close friend and fly-fishing buddy, a dentist in Claremont named "Doc" Hodgkins, telling me that Calvin Coolidge was "the best President we ever had."

In 1932, New Hampshire was one of the few states to agree with my father and support Harding, but Roosevelt swamped him anyway. Four years later the tide shifted, and the Granite State went for FDR the next three times, to my father's great consternation.

I never discussed politics with my mother when I was young, although I'm sure she considered herself a Republican. I do know that in her later years, after transplanting herself from Claremont to Boston, she became a registered Democrat. She voted for Bill Clinton and thought he was perfect, even when he wasn't.

I also know that at least once she did do wrong and voted for Roosevelt. My father never forgave her.

My Vertical Challenge and Passing the Beans

Growing up, I always thought height was a virtue. My mother would say of someone, "He's tall," in a tone of voice that made you know this was a good thing to be. Unfortunately, I never acquired that elevated status. Indeed, I never quite made it to five eight, stalling at five seven and a half.

My father was a short man, about five four. He used to say of me, when I was young, "He'll eat beans off my head." I don't know where he got that expression, which has always struck me as an odd thing to say.

I suppose I inherited my shortness from my father, along with a lazy eye and flat feet. And I seem to have passed my vertical handicap on to my three children, none of whom made it past five eight.

When I met the Pianist, a long time ago, I was conscious of the fact that she was taller. I would bemoan the disparity, and she would reassure me, "You're not short, you're medium." That made me feel a little better, though truth be told, not a lot.

Meanwhile, I've noticed that the vertical gap between us seems to be increasing.

"Stand up straight," she will say.

"I am," I tell her.

One day it dawned on me. She's not growing, I'm shrinking. First I lost the crucial half inch and fell to five seven even. Then five six and a half, again clinging to that extra half inch as if it made a difference. Now I fear it too may be gone. I'm not sure, however, and don't intend to find out.

The great poet, Robert Frost, once said that if he had to choose between increasing the height of people in New Hampshire or making the mountains taller, he would choose the latter. "The only fault I find with old New Hampshire," he wrote, "is that her mountains aren't quite high enough."

I disagree. Our mountains, beginning with Mount Monadnock, are just fine, thank you, but I could use a few more inches.

As the years passed, and I acquired grandchildren, I took to marking

Susie, Frank, Jacob, Ken, Sol, Liz,

off their growth by standing side-by-side to see how high they came up
on me. That isn't what you would call scientific measuring, but it's easier
than carrying a yardstick, and it suited my purpose. Jacob, my oldest
grandchild, moved up past waist, past shoulder, past ear, and now well
past top of head. At long last, a member of my family has attained the
virtue of being tall. It's time to pass the beans.

My Mother's Hobby and Roosevelt Grier

My mother had many interests. She collected antiques and would drive practically anywhere for an auction. I remember being dragged to some old lady's barn in Vermont, I think her name was Mrs. Harding, and hating every minute of it. My mother also volunteered for various causes—the hospital, the Red Cross, and other charities. And she liked certain games.

One was mahjong, a game of skill involving dice and tiles with Chinese letters, flowers, or symbols on them. It was popular starting in the 1920s, but I don't think it survived very far into the 1950s, at least in my mother's Claremont circle. Then there was canasta, a type of rummy game involving a tray, at least two decks of cards, and a lot of complicated rules. I actually learned how to play that game, but it, too, faded away at some point.

I don't recall that my mother played solitaire. These games were social events, but bridge was at another level entirely. It was serious business, and she and the ladies of the Claremont "Bridge Club" took no prisoners. I used to watch the games, just for a few minutes now and then, and was struck by the fact that it was completely incomprehensible and there was always someone called the "dummy."

My mother's lifelong hobby was needlepoint. I must have been a pretty negative kid because I couldn't see any value in that either. The needles looked like weapons, and the house was overrun with the products of all those patterns and yarn—pillows, footstools, wall hangings, and other useless stuff. I just thought it was a waste of time. Nothing you could play with, or even wear.

In 1970, long after she became a widow, my mother decided to leave Claremont and move to Boston. Her father, the grandfather who taught me about baseball and thought I was perfect, had recently died. She was approaching sixty, in good health, and ready for a new chapter in her life. So she put the house at Edgewood up for sale and located an apartment in the Prudential Center. She said she was going to get a job.

I explained to my mother that this was simply not realistic. First, she probably wouldn't be able to get a job, since she hadn't worked since her marriage nearly forty years before. Second, she really didn't have any marketable skills. If she did get a job, it would be doing something she didn't like. And, third, driving in Boston wouldn't be practical, so she would have to take the subway, and that would be a hassle.

At about that time, Roosevelt Grier, who had been a famous professional football player, appeared on television and let the public know that he had something in common with my mother: Needlepoint was his hobby. That created a bit of a needlepoint craze, just as my mother started job hunting.

It didn't take her long. She became the "Needlepoint Lady" of Lord & Taylor in Boston, a job she held for several years. She had the skill, she enjoyed demonstrating the process and selling the materials, and she didn't have to take the subway. Her building was next door to the store, and she could just walk across the plaza or, in bad weather, walk there underground. So much for having a know-it-all son.

My Ski Trips and a Very Good Sport

One recent winter was light on snow, and ski season was pretty much over when I ran into a friend of mine. He told me how much he and his family enjoyed their ski weekends at Gunstock—"Great skiing and no crowds," according to him. "Mostly man-made."

I got to thinking about our first ski winter, back when only God made snow. I think it was 1947, when I was eight. It seems like yesterday.

My mother was a good sport but no athlete. As I look back, I marvel at the fact that, when she decided my sister and I should learn to ski, she decided to learn too.

My mother drove us across the bridge from West Claremont to Mount Ascutney, where they had two ways of taking you up the hill: a rope tow for beginners and a snowcat for those courageous enough to go to the top. Our skis were long, straight, and made of wood.

I don't think my mother got very far beyond the "snowplow," and I wasn't much better; certainly not good enough to try out for the Stevens High School ski team. Besides, I preferred basketball, and I didn't want to risk getting hurt since I was always thinking ahead to the baseball season.

I told my middle-aged friend about my early days on skis. He confessed that he'd heard of rope tows but had never actually seen one. "You haven't missed anything," I told him, remembering the wet gloves and the aching shoulders. He said something about riding on a magic carpet. I had no idea what he was talking about.

After that first Ascutney winter, we went to a new ski area called Mt. Sunapee. They had rope tows too, but instead of a snowcat, there was a single-seat chair lift to get to the top. Going up, it felt like taking your life in your hands, and getting off was scary too. I still can't believe my mother did it. And she was old—nearly forty!

I still remember the names of the trails at Mt. Sunapee—Beck Brook, Hanson Chase, Lynx, Chipmunk (my favorite), and the dreaded Flying Goose, which I avoided.

A couple of years after that first Mt. Sunapee season, I went to Stowe with a friend, my first and only time there. We weren't old enough to drive, but my friend's mother took us in her white Cadillac. That was around the time the Trapp family opened their ski lodge, but the only sound of music we heard in Stowe was word that Josef Stalin had died. And someone broke into my friend's mother's room and stole all her jewelry, proving that not all hazards were on the slopes.

In later years, we skied at the usual places, and eventually I took my kids to many of them—Pat's Peak and Crotched Mountain nearby, Killington, Wilderness, and Sugarloaf farther afield. I never did take them to Suicide 6 in Woodstock, Vermont. I once got taken off that mountain on a ski patrol toboggan and swore I'd never go back.

I also gave up on Cannon Mountain. Going on the tramway the first time, I thought we were at the top only to see that there was another half a mountain still to go. The ride up was pretty, and a lot more secure than the old Mt. Sunapee chairlift, but when I got off I thought I was at the North Pole. Coming down was nothing but bumps. I kept wishing I was on the Chipmunk trail.

It has been a while since I went downhill skiing, and I don't know whether I will do it again. I do remember the day my mother's skiing career ended, to my great relief. It was on my sixteenth birthday in the winter of 1955. That was the day I got my driver's license.

My Mother's Decline and Words That Live On

There are different kinds of dementia, but the one we mostly hear about is Alzheimer's disease. One out of every eight Americans over sixty-five has this terrible illness. My mother was part of this unlucky group.

She had the usual symptoms—loss of memory, personality changes, general confusion—but she had the good sense to outwit the disease. Before it took away all her faculties, she died of something else.

Before those last few years, she was a formidable woman. As one of my sons says, "Mimi" (which is what her grandchildren called her) "had standards."

My mother as a nursing student, 1930

Growing up with such a mother wasn't always easy. For example, if I entered the house and the ladies of the sewing club were in the living room, I had to say hello to each of them *by name*. Another rule was that I couldn't leave the dinner table until everyone had finished eating. I would eat fast (I still do) in hopes that my parents and sister would do the same so I could go out and play.

One of the things I liked least was raking leaves. Everyone else raved about the fall foliage. I never really appreciated the colors until many years later in Jaffrey. We had a lot of trees on our land in Claremont (our address was fittingly named "Edgewood"), and as far as I was concerned, I was losing precious baseball time. I'm not saying I was abused, exactly, but you get the general idea.

My mother had a lot of great expressions, known in our family as "Irene-isms." I doubt that she made them all up, but most of them I haven't heard from anyone else. Of course I now find myself using them. It seems we all become our parents.

"Comparisons are odious," she would say, without explaining why that was so.

Speaking of "why," another was, "'Why' is a crooked letter," which was especially irritating to her curious son who asked too many questions.

Then there was "I don't deliver messages." I used to wonder, "Why not?"

Here's one from the pre-cell phone era: "I don't call long distance."

She had strong views about child-raising: "The love comes with the care."

I think I get that one, but "They're only lent to you for a little while?" Who "lent" me?

"I don't want the credit and I don't want the blame." Maybe she had doubts about how my sister and I would turn out.

Today, when children drink their milk or brush their teeth or clear the table, parents are likely to say, "Good job." That was definitely not one of my mother's expressions.

Those last two or three years were difficult. When the doctor told her that she had a tumor (it was pancreatic cancer, but I don't think he went into that much detail), she turned to my sister and me and came up with another great line, "As long as it's nothing serious."

My mother never wanted to leave her apartment in Boston, where she had lived since leaving Claremont in 1970, and with the help of caring home health aides, she never did. During her last year, I was traveling frequently between Boston and Puerto Rico. I would return to Logan Airport, go directly to her apartment, and call out, "It's your terrible, awful son."

I would enter her bedroom. By now she was a shadow of her former physical self. Yet she would say, "I don't have a terrible, awful son. I have a wonderful son."

Of all my mother's sayings, that one is my favorite.

Phyllis, our mother, and me on my first birthday, 1940

My Uncle Eddie and the Right to Brag

He was a son of New Hampshire. He was a member of the Greatest Generation. He helped save the world. He was my uncle, Edwin Firestone.

He was born in Littleton, New Hampshire, moved to Claremont, and graduated from Stevens High School in 1938. From there he entered Harvard College, "at age sixteen" my mother would always add. My mother, who was ten years older, believed there was one perfect person in the world—her brother Eddie.

After graduating from Harvard in 1942, he went to the Pacific as a Marine fighter pilot. My friends had family members in the War, but they were on ships, or on the ground. My uncle flew seventy-five missions over such places as the Solomon Islands and Guadalcanal. I knew I wasn't supposed to brag, but as a kid I couldn't resist telling my friends about my uncle the pilot. I made a model airplane, a Corsair, which is what he flew.

When he came back, he went to Florida as a flight instructor, and then I *really* had something to brag about: My uncle taught Ted Williams how to fly.

Yes—Ted Williams! And, when the war was over, and Ted returned to the Red Sox, my uncle took his father, my baseball-loving grandfather, to meet him and watch him play. I don't recall that my grandfather bragged about that. He was not one to single out one of his children over another. (The only bragging I ever heard from my grandfather, if you can call it that, was that "none of my children ever went to jail.")

Over the next sixty years, Uncle Eddie created a successful business in Boston, raised a family, saw his grandchildren (two sets of twins) grow to adulthood, and endured losses. He never gave my mother any reason to change her mind about his being perfect, with one possible exception. She loved to tell people that her brother's jewelry store, Firestone and Parson, was "in the Ritz Carlton Hotel." She was disappointed when he moved across the street, leaving her to say "His store is on Newbury Street, you know."

Uncle Eddie in the Solomon Islands, c. 1943

Left to right: Ed Firestone, Vincent Lipowsky, Charles A. Lindburgh, Henry G. Emery, Green Island, 1944. They all flew together that day.

He had many good qualities, including excellent judgment and the ability to make decisions quickly. One day, after my grandmother died, he came to Claremont to see my grandfather, who by then had lost most of his eyesight. "Dad," he said, "I think you need a new place to live."

By the end of *that day*, my uncle had bought the land, chosen the plans, and hired the builder. Later that year, my grandfather moved into a picture book-perfect house off Broad Street. From there, he could walk to the Pleasant Sweet Shop for coffee and conversation, as he did for several years.[4]

Uncle Eddie died on July 19, 2008, facing the end of life as he faced life itself—with strength, with courage, and with dignity. He knew his time had come, and he told me he was ready to go. The problem is that we were not ready for him to leave.

Maybe my mother was right about her brother being perfect. I'm still bragging about him.

My mother with her perfect brother

---

4   My mother helped furnish the new house and arranged the move. With his housekeeper Sadie as his scribe, my grandfather wrote a note to "my dear children," calling what they had done "the most marvelous thing that ever happened to me."

My Uncle Bill and Counting Points

My Uncle Bill was very short, a family trait on my father's side, and also very heavy. Actually, he was fat. Along with my father and a third brother, he worked at the shoddy mill in Claremont, which the three of them owned. He was a sweet man who never married, drove an Oldsmobile, smoked cigars, and loved going to the races at Rockingham.

Obesity has been in the news a lot lately. It's a big health problem in this country, the result of bad eating habits, fast foods, and sedentary lifestyles. Michelle Obama is trying to do something about childhood obesity with a program called *Let's Move*. She has even involved baseball players, although I'm a little upset with the selection of Yankees center fielder Curtis Granderson as the national chair. I'd have preferred David Ortiz. He is "Big Papi" after all.

When I entered high school, I weighed about 125 pounds, and the number has been creeping up ever since. At a certain point, somewhere between 140 and 150 pounds, this ceased to be a good thing, especially since I started out on the short side (though taller than my Uncle Bill) and in recent years have been getting shorter. Height is beyond my control, but pounds aren't. So, early in one summer I joined Weight Watchers. I wasn't terribly overweight, but I felt too heavy, and some of my clothes were starting to hurt. Paying the Weight Watchers fee for a few months is a lot cheaper than buying a new wardrobe.

For those of you who are not familiar with this program, they don't tell you what to eat, just how much. Everything is measured in points. Depending on your weight, age, and sex, you are allowed so many points per day. You can eat ice cream and chocolate cake and other indulgences, but it's not a good idea because you will quickly run out of points for the day. Exercise is good too. It can earn you extra eating points, maybe enough for a slice of pizza or a small piece of cake.

The question each morning is how to use points strategically. It was helpful that we had a bumper crop of blueberries in Jaffrey that summer, not to mention abundant fresh fruits and vegetables, all nutritious, good tasting, and low in points. I avoided pizza and cake but generally managed to reserve a place for two special points at dinner—a glass of wine or a lite beer.

By the fall, I weighed less, exercised more, and my clothes fit better. I even had to take some of them to the tailor. It all took me back to thoughts of my Uncle Bill. He used to come to our house for dinner, and I remember that he liked desserts. I don't think the words "diet" or "calories" were part of his vocabulary, and I doubt that he missed them. Maybe, back in his day, people simply accepted their bodies as they were, no questions asked.

My Uncle Bill called me "Yossel," the Hebrew name for "Joseph." He was the only person to do so, and I recently looked up the word. It means, "He will enlarge." Maybe my uncle knew something I didn't.

I don't remember whether Uncle Bill ate fruits or vegetables, but I doubt it, and I'm pretty sure he never ate eggplant. Too bad. It has no points.

My In-Laws and Healing Old Wounds

My father-in-law, Kal Ross, grew up in foster homes, enduring a dreadful childhood in New York City that left deep scars. My mother-in-law, Anita, lived in upstate New York all her life, if not in luxury then at least without the type of deprivation her husband had known. The two of them never, or hardly ever, exchanged a harsh word. She thought he was perfect, and he didn't mind that she felt that way.

I met them in 1961, when I was courting their daughter, Susan. They lived in a modest ranch house in Albany. Kal was out of work; Anita was nervous and apprehensive. They had a small circle of friends, pretty much kept to themselves, and enjoyed reading and watching TV.

He found work, she gave piano lessons. I married their daughter, the years passed, grandchildren arrived. Then, in 1983, my wife became ill and died. Their other child, a son, lived far away. Kal and Anita remained in their small house, family and friends provided what support they could, and they lived out the months and years, holding each other's hands.

Most families accumulate a history, and this one certainly did. Some of it was positive, some was not. There was tension with several relatives, including my father-in-law's father in New York. Given his unhappy childhood, I suppose you can't blame my father-in-law for feeling bitter. In this case it was pretty extreme. Until we went to see her grandfather at his apartment on the Grand Concourse in the Bronx, near the end of his life, my wife had never met him.

I'll never forget that visit. We rang the apartment's doorbell, he opened the door, and there was an older (and shorter) version of my father-in-law. He looked at his granddaughter, put his arms around her, and said, "I've always loved you."

There were problems with other family members too—slights, misunderstandings, failures of communication—not unlike most families. I was just a son-in-law, so I managed to remain a spectator to most of it. For others, however, lines were drawn. As we all learn sooner or later, Hallmark cards are mostly fiction.

Eventually my in-laws became frail, and he died at age 90. She was 93 but could still get up and play the piano. I always found it ironic that one of her favorite songs was *On the Sunny Side of the Street*. Apart from caregivers and the occasional visitor, she was mostly alone with her memories, hearing little, seeing less, remembering her lost ones.

She would have turned ninety-seven on July 4, 2007, a birthday she shared with the United States and one of its presidents, Calvin Coolidge, but she died that January. I last saw her a month before, when my son and I drove to Albany. She was still at home, and Frank thought she knew we were there. I wasn't so sure. We both realized that quality of life was no longer present, and her days were drawing to a close.

When you live to such an age, there aren't many friends left to attend the funeral. Still, the group was surprisingly large. Relatives came from California and Florida and North Carolina, as well as Boston and Albany, and a few friends came too—maybe twenty-five people in all. We gathered with sadness, but not grief. She was ninety-six, after all.

We went from the cemetery back to the house on Maxwell Street, and then a wonderful thing happened. Not fireworks, despite her birth date. Instead laughter, that precious commodity, started to fill the room. People who had not seen or spoken to each other in many years—cousins, uncles, in-laws—were glad to be together. It went on for the afternoon and into the evening. No one wanted to leave. It was, in other words, a celebration of life, as these events are meant to be.

Dinner at an Albany restaurant late that evening came down to six, the rest having departed for home. I'm sorry I wasn't at that dinner, but I heard about it the next day. "It was wonderful," my late wife's brother reported.

So, my mother-in-law accomplished in death something she was unable to do in life. She brought members of her family together, and she left all of us with a happy memory of the day we said good-bye.

My Bee Stings and the Tree Out Front

After my mother-in-law's funeral, when we went back to her house, family members came together, and old wounds were healed. This is a sequel to that story.

It goes back to 1991, or maybe back to 1961, when I first saw the nondescript house at 27 Maxwell Street in Albany and met my in-laws-to-be. Their daughter died in 1983, and I met the Pianist the next year. A few years later, my mother-in-law, Anita, said, "I hope you marry her."

I asked why, and she replied, "Because I don't think you'll find anyone else who will be as nice to me." I guess that's what's called having your priorities straight.

I took her advice. After we got married in 1991, the Pianist and I drove up to spend a few days at the house in Jaffrey we had bought five years earlier. One day we were clearing brush—not exactly the sort of thing one associates with a honeymoon—and I stepped in the wrong place and got stung by several bees. Within minutes I was in anaphylactic shock, and only due to the quick action of my new wife, a shot of epinephrine, and the attention of a local doctor named Ross Ramey am I here to tell the story. Ever since then, I have gone to the allergist every two months for desensitization shots. It has become part of my regular routine.

Meanwhile, my in-laws continued to live in the house on Maxwell Street. At a certain point in the history of Albany they must have had a sale on bricks, because everywhere you look, you see these brick houses. They look exactly alike, as if they were all designed and built by the same person on the same day.

Never much of a house to begin with, the house on Maxwell Street deteriorated with age, along with its occupants. It sits on a small patch of land, with one small tree between the house and the street. When my widowed mother-in-law died early in 2007, we worried that no one would buy it. The broker knew better, suggested an asking price that seemed much too high, and within a day or two the house was sold. I assumed that would be the last I would hear about it.

On one of my recent visits to the allergist's office, a new nurse appeared to administer my shots. We started to chat, and she told me she had recently moved to Boston from Albany, New York. I asked whether she knew Hackett Boulevard. She said she did.

I said, "Maxwell Street runs off Hackett."

"I know Maxwell Street," she replied.

"That's amazing," I said. "It is a very small street."

She explained that she knows the street because a dear friend of hers recently bought a "lovely" house there. That aroused my curiosity, and she told me that the old woman who lived there had died.

I knew, immediately, that it was number 27. "That old woman was my mother-in-law."

"Then you know the house," she said. "It's a great house," she went on, "and I just love the tree out front."

My Special Holiday and Perfect Grandchildren

This month we have Mother's Day, next month Father's Day, both time-honored holidays for parents, children, and the Hallmark Card Company. After the Fourth of July, we have breathing space until Labor Day, when we mark the end of summer by honoring workers and getting kids ready for school. Then, the following Sunday, we observe "Grandparents' Day." Well, "observe" may be the wrong word. More like "ignore."

I started thinking about the bond between children and grandparents a long time ago. My grandparents came from different villages in Russia and met in Boston, where she had a sister who was married to his cousin. They both spoke Russian and Yiddish and Polish, but beyond that, and the relatives, they had little in common except for their children and grandchildren.

Being a grandparent is a unique experience—less worry and responsibility than being a parent, yet brimming with love and hope for the future. A while back, a Russian-born cabdriver in New York asked me, "How come I love my grandchildren more than my children?" I thought for a minute and suggested that maybe he didn't love them "more," just "different."

"That's good," he said. "I'll tell my wife what you said."

My grandfather believed I was perfect. No one else has ever been guilty of that particular thought about me. I don't think he ever told me about his grandparents, but I tell my grandchildren about him, and the day will come when they will do the same with their grandchildren. That is our immortality.

Age thirteen is important for a Jewish boy or girl. It marks the coming of age when they become *bar* (or *bat*) *mitzvah*, "son" (or "daughter") of the commandments. When the day arrives, the child is called to the *bimah* (the elevated platform at the front of the sanctuary) to recite ancient prayers and receive blessings from parents, family members, and friends. This milestone means that the young person is no longer a child in the eyes of the community but rather a newly minted adult, morally responsible for his or her actions as a Jew and as a member of society.

I remember my *bar mitzvah* at Temple Meyer-David in Claremont. I remember the look on my parents' and grandparents' faces—such *nachas* (Yiddish for pride in one's children and grandchildren). My father told me about his coming of age, some forty-eight years earlier. I think back then they had to go from Claremont to Springfield, Massachusetts, in order to raise a *minyan* (the quorum of at least ten Jewish adults required for a service).

Not long ago, the press reported that the South African Judge, Richard Goldstone, would not attend his grandson's *bar mitzvah* in Johannesburg. Judge Goldstone, currently a visiting professor at Georgetown University, served as United Nations investigator of alleged war crimes in the conflict between Hamas and Israel, and many South African Jews were angry with him for placing much of the blame on Israel. It must have been with heavy heart that he agreed "in the interests of my grandson" not to attend the services because of the threat of protests.

As for the Sunday after Labor Day, "Grandparents' Day," I'm not going to worry about it. *My* 2010 grandparents' day will be May 22, the *bar mitzvah* date of my perfect grandson, Jacob. And, I'm happy to report, cooler heads have prevailed in South Africa. Judge Goldstone will be able to share this precious day with his grandson who, I'm sure, is also perfect.

My Daughter's Disclosure and Coming to Terms

One day, more than twenty years ago, my daughter Elizabeth and I were having dinner at a Chinese restaurant. "Dad," she said, "there's something I need to tell you." She paused, looked me in the eye, and said, "I'm gay."

I wasn't entirely surprised. I had suspected, but denial is a powerful force. I said very little.

"Are you sure?" I asked.

"Yes," she replied.

"How long have you known?"

"A long time," she said.

It felt like I'd been kicked in the stomach. I thought about the wedding that would not be, no walk down the aisle, no grandchild. In other words, I thought more about myself than about her.

She went to college, worked in Washington, then went back to school and became a nurse midwife. I don't think we discussed her "gayness." Part of me thought, or hoped, it would go away. The rest of me knew it wouldn't.

Some family members and friends found out or figured it out. I didn't talk about it, and as the years passed, I found myself thinking about it less, accepting it more. She met a wonderful woman, and they became partners. My daughter's happiness made me feel good, and the bonds between us kept getting closer.

Ten years ago, her partner died from a rare form of cancer called sarcoma. My sons and I went to the funeral in California. I felt like I had lost a daughter—a daughter-in-law?—and I felt a profound sadness for my daughter's loss. Gay or straight no longer mattered; all I wanted was for her to heal and find happiness in her life.

These past ten years have been challenging for my daughter—coping with loss, building a career, rebuilding a life. Fortunately, she is a strong and resilient woman. She is now a mother. My grandson Solomon was born in the fall of 2009. And she has met Janell, whom she likes and who likes her. I'm no longer fearful, as I was that night at the Chinese restaurant. I'm hopeful.

And so, I'm not looking back, today, I'm looking ahead. I'm now out of the parent's closet, and that is a good feeling. I was wrong about "no grandchild." Who knows? I may even yet get to walk my daughter down the aisle.[5]

---

[5] This piece was written in May of 2012. Janell and Liz are getting married in the summer of 2014.

My Unreserved Table and the Balloon Man

My grandson, Solomon, turned four recently, and I flew out to San Francisco for his birthday. My daughter had everything planned—the food, games, favors for the kids, even a "balloon man" to entertain by blowing up balloons and sculpting them into animals and cartoon characters. And the location was all set—a park near her house.

Soon after I arrived, I asked what I could do to help. "I called the Park Department to reserve the picnic table near the park's entrance," my daughter told me, "but they don't take reservations. It's first-come, first-served. Would you be willing to go over early and stake out the table?"

"I'll be glad to do that," I said. "What time is the party?"

"One o'clock," she said. "I was thinking I could drop you off around ten."

Three hours was more than I had expected, but getting that table was obviously important, and I had no other plans. "No problem, I'll take the Sunday paper," I said.

She dropped me off at exactly 10 a.m. We spread out a tablecloth and a few other things. My daughter went home to make frosting for the coconut cupcakes she had baked the night before. I went straight to the sports page.

Fifteen minutes later, a family arrived, carrying baskets and balloons. They looked over at me and my now-reserved table, shrugged, and headed over to the table near the swings and slides. I sent my daughter a text: "Just in the nick of time."

By noon I had read most of the newspaper, and I expected my daughter to show up at any minute. But before she did, another family arrived—parents, small daughter with eyes like saucers, grandparents, and a few other relatives. The father walked over to me and said, in a friendly way, "We have this table reserved."

"I'm sorry," I replied. "My daughter called and the city told her you can't reserve tables, it's first-come first-served. I got here more than two hours ago."

"I have a letter from the city," he said.

"I came all the way from Boston to reserve this table," I told him.

He nodded towards the older couple. "Those are my wife's parents. They came from India."

That stopped me, but only for a few seconds. "What part of India?" I asked.

Just then my daughter arrived, while I wondered where we were going to put twenty-two adults, twelve kids, and the balloon man. I didn't even think of what my grandson's namesake, King Solomon, would have proposed—splitting the table in two. I just looked at my daughter and said, "I think we're in trouble."

The man then produced the letter from the city, and, sure enough, he did have the table reserved. By then two things were clear. First, the Park Department had misinformed my daughter. And, second, these were really nice people. "How old is your daughter?" I asked.

"She's two, today" said the father. And then, pointing to the grandparents, "She's their first grandchild."

According to an old English maxim, possession is nine-tenths of the law, but I don't think that applied to our situation. I was ready to pack up and move, although I didn't know where.

Just then the father looked across the field and saw that the birthday group at the other table was packing up. "Look," he said, "the problem is solved. That table is available, and we'll be glad to use it." We protested, not too strenuously, but he insisted.

Later, my daughter left for a few minutes and came back with the father and his melt-your-heart birthday girl. They both enjoyed coconut cupcakes, and when they went back to her party she was carrying her own inflated Elmo, the furry Muppet from Sesame Street, courtesy of the balloon man.

Hon. Reginald C. Lindsay

People

My Partner Reg and Returning to Alabama

He was a law student, I was a young lawyer. We had a friend in common who told me, "You should meet this guy and your law firm should hire him." So I called and invited him for dinner. A year later, Reg came to work for the firm, Hill & Barlow.

His background was different from mine. He grew up in Birmingham, Alabama, during the 1960s. That was a lot different from my New Hampshire childhood a decade earlier. He went to Morehouse College in Atlanta, whose notable graduates included Martin Luther King, Jr. Morehouse is the only all-male historically black college in the United States. Oh, I forgot to mention another difference—Reg is black.

We worked together, we enjoyed each other's company, we played on the firm's softball team, he at third base, me at second. Reg was a natural athlete who (here's another difference) *did* make his high school baseball team. I dreaded a grounder to third with a runner on first, since that meant a throw from Reg to me, something like trying to catch a bullet.

He told me stories of his Alabama childhood. Some were funny, some were frightening. George Wallace was Governor, the notorious "Bull" Connor was in charge of "public safety," and fear walked the streets. Many whites, even those his age, called him "Boy." It was not a safe place to be a black teenager.

He also told me about his mother and his grandparents, who raised him in modest circumstances with unlimited love and faith. Reg told me that his grandfather was a wise man. One time they were approaching a railroad crossing in his grandfather's car. They heard the whistle of an approaching train, and his grandfather said, "You can beat the train, or the train can beat you. Just don't let it be a tie."

And he spoke about another wise man, Benjamin Elijah Mays, the president of Morehouse. He spoke at weekly chapel and urged his students to dream and to reach for the stars.

Reg did just that and entered Harvard Law School in 1967. He married Cheryl from Massachusetts and remained in Boston, a southerner by birth and a New Englander by choice.

Then, sometime in the late 1970s, Reg became ill. First he started to limp, and soon he was dragging one leg behind the other. The doctors probed and tested, but they couldn't come up with a diagnosis. Was it multiple sclerosis or, even worse, ALS, the disease nicknamed after the great baseball player, Lou Gehrig? They weren't sure, and Reg continued to deteriorate physically. This gifted athlete could hardly walk, much less play third base.

In 1983, spine surgery cured Reg's illness, but at a heavy cost. He left the hospital in a wheelchair and, despite physical therapy and rehabilitation, never regained the ability to walk. Yet, even with this handicap, he returned to our firm, where he had become a partner, and continued his career as a trial lawyer. Then, in the 1990s, he left the firm for a new job.

A few years ago, Reg received an invitation to return to Alabama. He accepted, and he did there what he had done for many years in Massachusetts. He presided at trials in the federal courthouse. Oh, there's one other thing I forgot to mention. Reg Lindsay's new job, the one for which he left the firm, was a Presidential appointment as a federal judge. This time, in Alabama, they called him "Your Honor."[6]

---

6 Honorable Reginald C. Lindsay died at Massachusetts General Hospital on March 12, 2009, at the age of sixty-three. Cheryl was with him, as were a few close friends, including me. I spoke at his funeral and shared some of the stories he told me. I have followed my grandfather's advice and remember him not in his last dark days but as he was.

My Lost Plane and Daniel Ellsberg

When I was ten, my parents gave me a wonderful present—a toy airplane with silver wings. It came with a small rod-and-reel retrieval device to keep the plane under control. On a windy New Hampshire spring day in 1949, I took the plane out for its first flight, and I lost it! It flew away, rod or no rod. I must have misread the instructions. I can still see the plane, untethered and birdlike, soaring into the sky.

I walked home, dejected, and looked at the box the plane came in. There was the name, Marx Toy Company, and an address. I sat down and wrote a letter, pouring out my ten-year-old broken heart.

Within a week or two a letter came from the Marx Toy Company. It wasn't a form letter from someone's assistant or a public relations representative, but a personal letter from the president of the company, Mr. Marx himself. It was a kind response, complimenting me on my well-written letter, suggesting that perhaps the directions could have been clearer, but pointing out that I should have attached the line to the rod before letting the plane out. Then came the best part: Mr. Marx promised to send me a replacement plane.

I waited for the plane to arrive. Days passed, then weeks. Finally, I told my mother that I wanted to write a letter to Mr. Marx to remind him to send the plane. She told me I could not write such a letter. Apparently she thought it undignified, a breach of an unwritten rule of etiquette that somehow only she knew. So, compliant child that I was, I wrote no letter, and I got no plane.

I told this story recently to Daniel Ellsberg, who was speaking about the Pentagon Papers case at an American Bar Association conference in California. In 1971, when Ellsberg leaked the papers to the *New York Times*, the press reported that he was married to Patricia Marx, Mr. Marx's daughter. I even thought, back then, of writing to her father to ask about my replacement plane, although more than twenty years had passed. But, once again, I didn't. Maybe I was still under my mother's influence; or maybe it just didn't seem like a proper thing for a Boston lawyer to do.

As I told the story, Ellsberg became animated and reacted to his late father-in-law's promise. "That sounds just like what he would do," he told me.

When I got to the point where the plane didn't arrive, he said, "You should have written him another letter."

I told him the rest of the story, that I wanted to but my mother wouldn't let me. His face dropped. Daniel Ellsberg, fifty-seven years after my plane flew away, shared my lingering disappointment. He asked for my card, gave me his, and told me he would tell the story to Pat when he got home.[7]

---

7 This was my first piece published in the *Monadnock Ledger-Transcript*, and I sent a copy to Daniel Ellsberg. A few weeks later, he sent me his book, *SECRETS: A Memoir of Vietnam and the Pentagon Papers*, inscribed:
"6-27-06 To Joe, for peace and truth—and to restore the honor of Marx Toys and my wife's father. Dan Ellsberg"

My Blind Friend and Crossing the Street

He grew up on the other side of New Hampshire, a good athlete but an indifferent student. If he was smart, he didn't realize it. Then came the diagnosis of diabetes. Incurable, yes, but one can live with it, and he did.

After Somersworth High School, he worked at various jobs, construction mostly, and then the diabetes took a turn for the worse—diabetic retinopathy. He was losing his sight. That pretty much eliminated employment, at least what he had been doing.

New Hampshire offers help for anyone in such a predicament, and he took advantage by enrolling at Keene State. He spent a year there and discovered that he wasn't such a bad student after all. He was completely blind by then, and getting around a small town was difficult.

Cities have their drawbacks, but at least they provide public transportation. So, now in his mid-twenties, he applied to Boston College. Three years later he graduated with honors.

"Going blind was the best thing that ever happened to me," he said later. "It opened my eyes."

He entered Boston College Law School the next fall. When he arrived, an adviser suggested a reduced course load the first year. "Law school is pretty daunting," the adviser told him, "even for those with 20-20 vision."

"No way," he said. "I don't want any favors, and I can handle it."

And he did. By second year he was in the top third of the class. Mostly he read with the latest technology, machines that translate the written word into speech. He chose not to learn Braille because he was in a hurry and considered it too slow.

That's where I come in. He applied to my firm for a summer job between his second and third years, and I was in charge of hiring. He and his seeing-eye dog took the "T" into downtown Boston for an interview, and he told me about himself.

I asked, "If it would take a seeing person an hour to figure out a legal problem, how long would it take you?"

He gave me the perfect answer to a dumb question: "Fifty minutes."

He joined us for that summer, and after graduating a year later he came to work for the firm fulltime. He took an apartment on Beacon Hill so he could walk to work, another example of his remarkable courage. Have you ever tried to cross the street in downtown Boston?

He worked hard, and his determination never waned, even in the face of a kidney transplant along the way. When the firm closed its doors in 2002, he returned to New Hampshire and practiced law in Concord. One of his specialties was healthcare law. Who could be better qualified?

He was tough as nails. He never sought sympathy, and he never felt sorry for himself.

One time he told me, "If I could have my sight back, I wouldn't take it."

I'm not sure why he felt that way, but I think it had to do with how full his life became after he lost what most of us take for granted.

Peter Callahan died in Somersworth, New Hampshire, on July 23, 2007. He was forty-two. Even a spirit as large as his could not overcome the ravages of diabetes.

He was a dear friend. He was a noble son of New Hampshire. He will always be one of my heroes.

My Birthmate and the Phenomenon of Email

Email has become a type of addiction. You send one and a reply comes back in a minute, as if the person was just sitting at the computer or looking at his handheld device waiting to hear from you. Even worse, if you don't reply to an email the minute it arrives, the sender sends another one asking "Didn't you get my email?" My favorite is when you check your email after breakfast, and someone has sent you an email in the middle of the night. Maybe it's the new way of counting sheep.

For a while I was getting a lot of junk email. Even with the benefit of filtering software, a certain amount of it still gets through. There's this lady in Nigeria who says that her late husband, the deputy minister of something, left her with fifty million dollars and now she wants me to help make "arrangements." I think I'll pass.

Then there is the helpful service that wants to improve a certain part of my anatomy. No thanks to that one too.

A boy named Tony Dempsey and I were born on the same day in February, a long time ago. Claremont General Hospital had only one delivery room, and his mother got there first. So my mother and I had to settle for a regular hospital room, a fact I've used from time to time as an excuse—"Well, what did you expect? I didn't even get the delivery room when I was born."

Tony and I used to celebrate our birthdays together, but he moved away when we were in kindergarten and I never heard from him again. Until recently.

This childhood friend who had disappeared from my life looked me up on the Internet. He sent an email telling me that he lived in California, remembered our early years together in Claremont, and was eager to catch up.

I replied and told him I remembered him.

"You wore rimless glasses," I wrote.

He replied, "Yes, and I still do."

One thing led to another, and he said he would like to come east and see me and some others from those days. It happened that our Stevens High School fiftieth reunion was coming up, and he thought that would be a good time to return. Here he was, a Californian who never attended Stevens or any other Claremont school, unless you count kindergarten at the Bluff School. And this "outsider" was proposing to travel across the country and intrude on "our" reunion.

He wanted to know, what did I think? I didn't want to tell him that I thought this was another weird email, so I said something like, "It would be wonderful to see you, but it's a long trip." He took that as a positive response.

Tony came to the reunion, with his wife, and his long-ago playmates from the neighborhood known as "the Bluff" had an experience that one doesn't expect in life. We reconnected with someone we had lost early in our lifetimes. More than sixty years had passed, and I'm not saying we filled in all the gaps. But someone cared enough about those shared early years to send an email, make that long trek, and take that considerable risk. As far as I'm concerned, anyone who does what he did deserves to be an honorary member of the Class of '57.[8]

Five old friends from the Bluff, June 2007 Left to right; Dolina Miller, Joyce Colby Buswell, Tony Dempsey, Jane Ufford Bartlett, me

8 After finding me in 2006, Tony emailed me every year, addressing me as "my younger friend." He did so on February 19, 2010, telling me he was "battling lymphoma." On our birthday the next year, I was in San Francisco visiting my daughter. I told her about my birthmate, who lived in California. "Every year he emails me," I told her. "This year I'm going to beat him to the punch. I'm in his time zone for a change." So I called and wished Tony a happy birthday. He mentioned that he'd had a setback but was optimistic, and we had a good chat. He died less than a month later, on March 12, 2011.

My Friend Luis and the Extended Warranty

Luis Molina died last year at the age of 101 and a half. If you get to such an age, you're allowed to add the fraction, just as young children do when we ask their age. In the case of Luis, old age was nothing like what Shakespeare had in mind when he described the seven ages of man. Luis never lost his charm or his keen intellect. Anyone who thinks you're supposed to slow down when you move to "Assisted Living" didn't know Luis. To the very end he was, to quote his friend Polly Gottschalk, "sharp as a tack."

He was born in Boston, educated at Harvard, and lived much of his life in Connecticut, where he rose through the ranks of a large insurance company. Music was essential to Luis. He was a proficient pianist, sang in the Harvard Glee Club, and never missed a concert.

I've noticed a connection between music and longevity. The only other centenarian I've known, Dr. A. Stone Freedberg, also died last year at the age of 101 and a half. Like Luis, he was passionate about music. Friends gave him a concert for his one-hundredth birthday, and I ran into him at Symphony Hall the following year.

The Pianist says I should add the American composer Nicolas Slonimsky, who also lived to 101 and a half. I didn't know him, but she did. Then I did a little research and found that Irving Berlin (whom neither of us knew) did the same thing. Maybe we should all write music, or at least go to more concerts.

After moving to Peterborough with his wife Kay in 1997, Luis immersed himself in the cultural life of the Monadnock region. He chaired the Performing Arts Committee of the RiverMead retirement community in Peterborough and lent his considerable energies to promoting cultural activities and supporting local arts groups—Apple Hill Chamber Music, Monadnock Music, Peterborough Players, and probably others I don't know about. Luis never looked back. For him, it was always about the next day, and the day after that.

I remember running into Luis in 2004, when he was a mere ninety-six. "I just bought a new car," he told me.

"What kind?" I asked.

"A Hyundai," he answered.

Luis then explained the terms of the purchase. "It comes with a four-year warranty, but if you pay more you can get six years."

I took the bait. "Which did you get?"

"Oh, I got the six years," Luis said.

At some point Luis gave up driving. I don't know whether he made it into the fifth year of the warranty. I don't suppose it matters. What does matter is that even during the tenth and eleventh decades of his life, he remained optimistic, lived life to the fullest, and listened to music every day.

My Partner Dave and a House in Jaffrey

One Friday in 1986, my partner Dave came by my office and said, "I've been thinking you should get a house."

He and I both lived in Boston, he had bought a house on the Cape, and I guess he thought I needed one too, along with a mortgage. After all, what are partners for? I had been to Cape Cod (in Boston they say "down the Cape"), and it wasn't for me. Too much traffic.

That night I told the Pianist about the conversation. "Just suppose you wanted a house," she said. "Would you go back to Lake Sunapee?"

I said no. When I was young, my family had a cottage in Perkins Cove, near the state park beach, and we spent many happy summers there. But that was from another time, and I was content with my memories.

The conversation might have ended there, but it didn't. I mentioned that the Monadnock area was supposed to be nice, although that was mostly rumor. I wasn't quite sure where it was—near Keene, I thought.

I picked up the *Boston Globe* from the kitchen counter and glanced at the real estate section. The stars must have been aligned just right because I spotted an ad from a Peterborough broker with the word "Monadnock" in it. Purely on a whim, I called the broker, whose name was Hilda Weatherbee, introduced myself, and lied.

"I'm interested in a house," I told her.

She asked me what sort of house I had in mind, but since I hadn't given it a minute's thought, I didn't have a ready answer. Finally I said, "Nothing fancy."

I thought I could hear her frowning over the phone, but she was cordial. "Can you be a little more specific?" she asked.

"Well," I said, "maybe a place with a view."

At that point, realizing I'm sure that she was dealing with someone who didn't know what he was talking about, she invited us to come up and look around. I covered the phone and asked the Pianist, "How about a trip to New Hampshire tomorrow?" She nodded yes.

"Hilda, are you free tomorrow," I asked.

She paused for what seemed like quite a while and then said, "Sure."

Mount Monadnock from our dock on Gilmore Pond

This was long before GPS, but with the help of a roadmap, we drove to Peterborough the next morning, and Hilda took us to see four houses. The first was on a lake in Hillsborough, where I had worked at a camp a long time ago. Two were in Jaffrey, where I'd never been. And one was a log cabin in Rindge.

"There isn't much on the market right now," Hilda explained, "but if you decide you are really interested, we can keep looking. I'm sure more houses will become available."

So there we were, having invested a morning in this lark in the country. I asked the Pianist, "Which house did you like?"

"The second one," she answered. "Which one did you like?"

"I liked the second one too," I replied.

After a pause, I turned to Hilda. "We'll take the second one."

"Just like that?" she asked.

"Just like that," I answered.

And that's how we got to Jaffrey. Thanks, Dave. We like it here.

Our Neighbor and the End of an Era

According to her obituary, she was born in Massachusetts in 1919. I don't question the accuracy of that report, but there is a larger truth. The article says as much: "She was a lifelong resident of Jaffrey." In fact, Elinor Moore was Jaffrey to the very core.

When we first saw what was to become our Jaffrey house, we also met Miss Moore. Within moments after we pulled into the driveway, she appeared, just to see who was nosing around. I should have mentioned Ellie when I wrote about that visit and my on-the-spot decision to buy the house on Gilmore Pond. We have never regretted that decision, not even for a New York minute.

Ellie lived in a small unit attached to the red barn across the street. Starting on that first day, and for the next twenty years, she was our neighbor, our helper, our friend, and our historian. She knew everything about "the Cann house," as it was then, and still is, known. And she knew about many subjects—flowers, birds, gardens, and the town. She was a virtual Jaffreypedia.

Ellie had a basic goodness about her that we don't see very often. She was not impressed by wealth or status. She liked people who were fair, honest, and hardworking, not "shiftless" as she put it. "She was a nurse's aide," the obituary reported, which somehow doesn't quite tell the whole story.

When we first met her, she was helping our neighbor, Marion Mack Johnson, who lived nearby and had owned our house before Mr. Cann. She later took care of others in the town, striking out each morning in her bright red car, stopping off at the post office on her way. For those she helped, she was a cheerful, undemanding person. She liked to chat, and to reminisce. Beyond that, she asked very little.

For us, she was a godsend. With her across the road, we didn't need an alarm system. She kept an eye out and would call us in Boston if she saw anything that didn't look quite right.

And she knew where everything was. If she hadn't shown us how to turn off the outside water, our pipes would long since have frozen. She helped take care of our lawn until she "retired" several years ago. She kept us informed of the latest town happenings. She and the Pianist had a great friendship, sharing a love of flowers and gardening.

Over the years she told us about her parents, especially her mother, and about the family's poultry farm. She claimed that her fingers were crooked because of all the cows she milked when she was young.

Once or twice she mentioned the beau she had a long time ago. Apparently the family didn't approve, and that was that—she remained "Miss" Moore. We never got the details.

As age took its toll, she could no longer live on her own, so she lived out her last two years in a nursing home. We saw her there from time to time, but it wasn't the same. She was still alert, glad to see us, but the life she had led was no longer. Ellie loved animals and missed her cat terribly. At the end of our visits, she always walked us to the elevator and, once or twice, went down with us and checked on the pet rabbit out front.

She lived a long life, eighty-nine years, and now that she has gone, a part of the town has gone with her. The obituary noted, "A graveside service will be held at a later date at the family lot in Conant Cemetery, Jaffrey." We were there, and I had the honor of reading this piece.

My Neighbor Malcolm and the Naming of Houses

Back in the mid-1980s, Mildred and Malcolm Freiberg considered buying the Cann House on Gilmore Pond Road but decided to pass. They did us a favor. The house was still available when we stumbled upon it and became its owners, in 1986. The Freibergs decided, instead, to build a house on the other side of the pond. That was another favor to us. They became our neighbors and, over time, our dear friends.

That side of the pond lost two remarkable citizens in less than two years. First, Malcolm's friend and neighbor, Harvard economics professor Jim Duesenberry passed away. Jim died in the fall of 2009 at the age of ninety-one. And then Malcolm died on June 27 at the same age.

Malcolm's last visit to Jaffrey, a place he loved dearly, was on Memorial Day weekend, just a few weeks before his death. Over the years, he attended lovingly to his vegetable garden, usually outwitting the critters and producing tomatoes that he enjoyed sharing as much as eating. We learned at the funeral that Randy Miller had the ground ready, just in case Malcolm was up for planting this year.

Malcolm did more than tend to his garden. He tended to his family and his friends, with loyalty and great affection. They responded in kind. With him, unassuming person that he was, it was never about "me," it was always about "you."

He was nearly two decades older, but we shared quite a bit. We both went to Brown University, but he was there under the G.I. Bill to obtain a Ph.D. I'm not sure I ever heard him talk about his wartime service in Europe, for which he received a Bronze Star. (Did I mention his modesty?) Another thing we shared—we both married pianists. And we were of the same religion and held similar political outlooks. In other ways we were quite different, he with his mustache and mutton chops and restrained manner, I with none of those.

"Choose life," the Old Testament directs us. Malcolm did so, and more. First as a teacher, and then as an editor at the Massachusetts Historical Society, he helped generations of students and scholars gain a better understanding of American history.

Life was not always kind. He suffered great sadness and loss—the deaths of a daughter many years ago, and his dear Mildred in 2006. But he didn't just choose life, he *embraced* it, and life reciprocated in kind, blessing him in his later years with grandchildren whom he cherished. On the one hand life takes, on the other hand it gives.

Near the end, just inches from death, Malcolm apologized that he was unable to get up and greet a visitor who had come to see him. I don't speak Yiddish, but my grandparents and parents did, and I picked up a few words along the way. One of them is *mensch*, which is used to describe a person of integrity and honor. It describes Malcolm better than any other word I can think of.

We still own the "Cann House." Even with a new paint job and a new roof, nothing can change the name of our house. Meanwhile, the house across the pond will always be the "Freiberg House." It could also be called the "*Mensch* House."

My Jaffrey Neighbor and the Last Flight

Oh! I have slipped the surly bonds of Earth
And danced the skies on laughter-silvered wings;
Sunward I've climbed, and joined the tumbling mirth
Of sun-split clouds—and done a hundred things
You have not dreamed of . . .
    "High Flight," by John Gillespie Magee

People like Peter Reed don't come along every day. He could do many things, but what he liked best was building model airplanes. For those of you who don't know any modelers, they are a breed apart. I built model airplanes as a kid, but what Pete did bore no resemblance to my childhood pastime. He was a true craftsman.

He was up by five every morning and began each day, from early spring to late fall, with a dip in Gilmore Pond. He never had time on his hands. When he wasn't in his shop, he was reading, watching sports, listening to music, or engaged in other activities. There simply weren't enough hours in the day.

For Pete, it had to be just right, whether it was a replica of a World War II fighter plane (even the insignias had to be authentic), the restoration of an ancient canoe, or building a new raft for his next-door neighbors.

He loved the country and hated cities. After watching the Red Sox go down to their third and last defeat in the 2009 playoffs, we were talking about life, as we often did, and I asked him whether he had a favorite city.

"Absolutely not," he replied. "I hate 'em all."

A few minutes later, he told the Pianist he had been thinking about a concert he attended last summer and wondered if she could define "music" for him in fifty words or less. They must have talked for at least a half hour.

Several years ago, Pete came down with an illness called amyloidosis. This is a rare disease that you don't want to have. He took it in stride, even the lengthy treatment at Boston Medical Center, in a city he didn't like despite the fact that he was born there. He withstood the unpleasant side-effects and bounced back, nearly as good as new. He had more airplanes to build and fly.

He was well-known in the model airplane world, traveling to states all around the country for meets. He was a pillar of the National Miniature Pylon Racing Association and a member of the Aviation Model Hall of Fame. He had a network of flying buddies everywhere. He loved them, and they loved him.

On October 14, 2009, he got up and announced, "It's a beautiful day." With fruit and a sandwich packed for lunch, he drove off to Connecticut for a meet. He got there, put a plane in the air, fell to the ground and died of a heart attack.

It doesn't do justice to leave it that Pete built airplanes that are works of art. He had an even greater skill. He built friendships. I never asked him to teach me how to build airplanes, but I learned a lot from him. By his example, he taught me how to live a fuller life.

We lost a dear friend, and the best neighbor ever. Jaffrey lost one of its finest citizens. Thanksgiving that year was saddened by his absence, but sweeter for having had him in our lives.

My Dearie Friend and a Life Fully Lived

I met her for the first time nearly forty years ago. My law partner, Bob Johnson, the person who years later introduced me to the Pianist, was her lawyer. He asked me to join him for breakfast at her house in Cambridge to discuss a problem. Someone was selling dolls that looked like her. I was so excited I could hardly sleep the night before. When I got there, she, her husband Paul, and I went into her back yard. I'll never forget that meal—tea, grapes, and toast.

Julia and me, 1994

The Pianist had provided the music for one of her television series. When we got married fifteen years after that breakfast, she came to our wedding party. A young man just getting started in the catering business provided the food. Six years later, on the occasion of her eighty-fifth birthday, he was one of the chefs at a benefit dinner in her honor.

He reintroduced himself. "You won't remember me," he said, and told her he had catered our dinner several years earlier.

She paused for only a second or two, looked down, and replied, "Lamb chops!" She was right, of course.

One day in 1994, she told me she was going to her sixtieth reunion at Smith College. I made one of my less sage remarks, "I'll bet you're the most famous person in your class."

"I believe I am!" she said.

She never endorsed a product. Whenever a company tried to sell food or wine or even computers by using her name or her look or her unique sound, she pounced. This happened several times, and the result was that the transgressor paid some dollar amount for the offense, and she gave the money to her favorite charity, the American Institute of Food and Wine.

Then she would say to me, "I do hope they do it again soon. The Institute needs the money, you know."

She came to our office several times to have lunch with the summer associates, students entering their last year of law school. We served cold cuts, and she told them about her life. "I'm too busy to spend time cooking; I usually get take-out," one young man told her.

"That's not eating," she said, "that's *feeding*."

One time she needed legal help in California. I contacted a lawyer in San Francisco, who asked what it was about. I said we first needed to clarify the fee arrangement. Trying to sound serious, I said "Your fee is that you get to go to a very good restaurant with the client."

The lawyer asked who the client was. When I answered the question, the response was immediate. "It's a deal."

Another time we were co-auctioneers for a Monadnock Music fundraiser in Peterborough. Driving back to Cambridge, we talked about life and work. She was eighty-two at the time, and I asked whether she planned to retire.

"Yes," she told me, "when I'm old."

"When is that?" I asked.

"When I'm eighty-eight," she answered.

She moved from Cambridge to Santa Barbara in 2002. On her way, she took a detour and spent a week in the town of Napa, California, to help her friend Robert Mondavi dedicate The American Center for Wine, Food and the Arts. My daughter was living in Napa, and she told me where she was staying and that my daughter should give her a call, and they would get together for lunch.

My daughter made the call, and they agreed on a place and time. Just so my daughter would not have a problem knowing which one she was, she said "I'll be the tall woman wearing the purple blouse."

She often called people she liked "Dearie," but she was the dear one—Julia Child.

My Summer Movies and Julia Child's Friend

Julia Child lived in Cambridge, had a home in Southern France, and died in California, the state of her birth. She shared herself with a vast audience, including the people of New Hampshire. She helped raise money for New Hampshire charities such as Monadnock Music, and visited her dear friend Lael Wertenbaker in Keene.

Julia and Lael met in Europe during World War II, when Julia was with the Office of Strategic Services and Lael was a war correspondent for *Time* magazine. Maybe they were both spies.

Julia died on August 13, 2004, just two days short of her ninety-second birthday. Five more years and she could have seen a movie called *Julie and Julia*, which opens tomorrow. Meryl Streep plays Julia, and Stanley Tucci plays her husband Paul. They are good actors, but there was something so unique about Julia, and Paul too, that it's hard to imagine anyone stepping into their shoes.

I call her "Julia" because all of us who knew her did so. For that matter, not even strangers called her "Mrs. Child." In that sense, everyone knew her. But I was one of the lucky ones who actually did know Julia Child.

Julia was special in many ways, and not just how she looked and how she sounded. She did one thing—educating the public about food and how to cook it—and she did it better than anyone else before or since. She changed the way America thought about food, and how America ate. She was larger than life on television, and in real life too. No one ever felt she was talking down to them although, given her height of six foot two, she usually was. And the voice! She always seemed nearly out of breath, but never at a loss for words.

Julia's friend, Lael Wertenbaker, was also a remarkable woman. During the War, she interviewed many notables, including the Nazi leader Joseph Goebbels. She knew most of that era's famous people, including Orson Welles. Like Julia, she was one of a kind.

I met Lael only once, near the end of her life, at a charity auction in New Hampshire where I was Julia's co-auctioneer. Lael told me about her career as a journalist reporting from Berlin at the beginning of the war. I later learned of her many books on subjects as varied as her husband's death (*Death of a Man*), the life of Mata Hari, who definitely *was* a spy (*The Eye of the Lion*), and cardiac surgery (*To Mend the Heart*). She came to the MacDowell Colony in Peterborough to write, and moved to New Hampshire in the 1960s.

Lael never had a movie made about her, but there was a play on Broadway in 1962 called *A Gift in Time*. It was based on Lael's book about her husband's death, and Olivia de Havilland played Lael. Olivia (I'll use her first name even though I don't know her), was born in 1916 and is the last living star from *Gone with the Wind*. She won two best actress Academy Awards and, in 2008, the National Medal of Arts.

So who's the "Julie" depicted in this new movie? From what I've read, she cooked all the recipes in Julia's *Mastering the Art of French Cooking* and wrote a blog on the subject. No small feat, to be sure, and Amy Adams probably does a good job portraying her. I don't know Amy either, but I've seen her in a movie or two and I'll tell you this: She's no Olivia de Havilland, and Julie's no Lael Wertenbaker. As for Meryl Streep, we'll see how she does as Julia, but I do know this: She's eight inches shorter!

Julia and the Pianist, 2002

My Friend Dick and the Epidemic of Man-Made Disasters

There are two types of disasters—natural and man-made. We seem to be having an epidemic of both. This column is about the latter, the disasters that people, mostly powerful men it seems, bring upon themselves.

Of course this is nothing new. Gary Hart wanted to be President but got caught with Donna Rice doing "Monkey Business" on a boat of that name. Then there's Bill Clinton, who apparently couldn't resist Monica, the young intern with the blue dress.

You'd think public figures would have learned from the mishaps of others, but somehow oversized egos get in the way of undersized common sense, and not just in our country. We've been hearing for years about Italy's Prime Minister, Silvio Berlusconi, whose 24/7 amorous capers have been eclipsed by the allegations against his French compatriot, Dominique Strauss-Kahn, whose fall from the echelons of power happened literally overnight.

Eliot Spitzer paid to play and had to resign as New York's Governor. Nevada's John Ensign quit the Senate after being outed as a complete cad. His bizarre story includes a payment by his parents, of all people, to the Senator's former chief of staff with whose wife the Senator was having . . . well, you get the idea. Arnold Schwarzenegger is another recent case, although the surprise is more that the "love child" was kept secret for so long than that he existed. Maybe the Terminator can find a role for John Edwards in his next movie. Between the two of them, they could start their own "birther" movement.

I don't know any of these people, or Tiger Woods either, but I do know Dick Morris. We met on a beach in Aruba back in the late 1970s. He told me that he was in the political campaign business, and that he had worked on Bill Clinton's Arkansas campaigns. I asked Dick when he was going to run a presidential campaign.

"When Bill Clinton runs for President," he told me.

Over the following years, I saw Dick from time to time, either in New

York or in Massachusetts, where he was an adviser to Governor Weld. For some reason, Dick wasn't visible when Clinton ran for President the first time, but he was in the thick of the re-election campaign, serving as the President's campaign manager.

Then disaster struck. Dick got caught on a hotel balcony with a member of the world's oldest profession, and he resigned from the campaign. Dick's picture was on the cover of *Time* magazine two weeks in a row, pre- and post-balcony.

I decided I should give Dick a call. What are friends for, after all? His wife, Eileen, answered the phone, Dick came on the line, and I realized that I hadn't planned what to say. I could have quoted the last line of the movie *Some Like It Hot* ("Well, nobody's perfect"), but that didn't occur to me. Instead I came up with these priceless words: "We all make mistakes."

"Yes, Joe," said Dick, who grew up in New York City, "but I made mine in Macy's window."

America is the land of second chances, and Dick Morris has long since come back in full force. He writes books and articles, appears regularly on Fox News, and gives advice to politicians. All in all, Dick serves as a role model for others who have run afoul of moral sensibilities. So does former New York Governor Spitzer who, soon after resigning from office, became the host of a nightly television show on CNN. Maybe former Senator Ensign has a future on the Animal Planet channel. Before politics, he was a veterinarian.

My Supreme Court Count and Justice Souter

Much has been written about David H. Souter. There is more coming, no doubt, as legal scholars look back on his career as a member of the United States Supreme Court and, before that, the New Hampshire Supreme Court. According to a recent article in the *Boston Globe*, he is "the last New Englander." I'm not sure what that means, but it doesn't sound right to me. The same article says he is "only the second Supreme Court justice from New Hampshire, following by 145 years the appointment of Levi Woodbury."

I don't mean to nitpick, but that's not right either. And I don't like to see New Hampshire shortchanged. It's true that Levi Woodbury was from New Hampshire. He was born in Francestown in 1789, the same year the Constitution was adopted. Like Justice Souter, he had a distinguished public career. Woodbury was Governor at age thirty-four, went on to the United States Senate, became Secretary of the Navy and Secretary of the Treasury, and then returned to the Senate. When President Polk named him to the nation's highest court in 1845, he became the first person to have served as a governor and in all three branches of government.

Only one other person has accomplished that quadfecta—Salmon P. Chase. He was born in Cornish, which we considered a suburb of Claremont when I was growing up. By my reckoning that makes him "from New Hampshire." True, after graduating from Dartmouth he moved to Ohio, and he was later elected to various state and federal positions from that state. Abraham Lincoln defeated him at the 1860 Republican National Convention, appointed him Secretary of the Treasury as one of the "team of rivals" recounted in Doris Kearns Goodwin's book of that name, and appointed him Chief Justice in 1864.

There was another justice between Woodbury and Chase, a portly fellow named Nathan Clifford. He was born in Rumney, home of the Polar Caves up in Grafton County. He practiced law in Maine and went on to become a member of Congress, Attorney General, and United States Envoy to Mexico. President Buchanan appointed him to the

Supreme Court, where he served for over twenty-three years.

I'm not done. The *Boston Globe* also forgot about Harlan Fiske Stone, born in Chesterfield, right here in Cheshire County. President Coolidge appointed him to the Supreme Court in 1924, and President Roosevelt made him Chief Justice in 1941. He was number four.

Maybe what the *Boston Globe* really meant was that Justice Souter was the second Supreme Court Justice from *Hillsborough County*. But that's not quite right either. He does live in Weare, but he was born in Massachusetts.

Justice David H. Souter at Harvard Law School

My Friend's Son and Flag Burning

In June of 1989, the Supreme Court ruled that flag-burning is "expressive conduct" protected by the First Amendment. Despite repeated Congressional efforts to overrule that case by constitutional amendment, it remains the law today.

In August of that year, I was visiting an Elderhostel camp in Maine, where the Pianist was helping senior citizens improve their piano skills. The owner asked if I would like to speak to the "campers" about a legal subject. He suggested estate planning. I told him I knew nothing about wills or trusts and offered to talk about flag burning instead. He didn't look too happy but acquiesced.

That evening, I explained the Court's reasoning to thirty or so senior citizens. At the beginning of my talk, I asked how many of them believed that flag burning should be a constitutional right. Only a few hands went up. A half hour or so later, I asked the same question. More hands went up this time, but many of these senior citizens remained unconvinced.

Over the following Thanksgiving weekend, a professor friend and his son came to visit. The father had marched at Selma and protested the Vietnam War. The son's patriotism was of a different sort. He had graduated from a military high school and was attending a prominent military college.

I told them about my visit to Maine and the subject of my talk. The son was not just unconvinced. He was outraged that the Supreme Court would ever make such a decision. I said something about the Constitution and freedom of speech, and then I saw the two of them looking at each other in a way that told me I had stumbled onto something. And I had.

It seems that just a few weeks before, the young soldier-to-be had visited his father's office on the college campus. He looked out the office window, saw smoke, and was shocked to see students burning a flag. How could anyone do such a thing?

Without saying a word, he broke into the fire extinguisher case in the hallway and ran down three flights of stairs. When he got there, the fire was out and the students were gone. The campus police apprehended him, took the extinguisher, and cited him for breaking the glass since there was no "emergency."

As the story came out at my kitchen table, the son sat quietly, his head bowed, while the father told me that he had been embarrassed by his son's behavior and not stood up for him. I pointed out that expressive conduct can take more than one form. They both fell silent, and then the father got up, kissed his son, and said he was proud of him.

The next week I sent them both a copy of the Supreme Court's opinion. I don't remember the professor's response, but I will never forget the son's. He sent me a kind note, thanked me for the opinion, and enclosed his own gift in return—an American flag.

My Commute and the Gift of Life

Commuting by public transportation offers several opportunities. You can read the newspaper or a book. You can start the workday by doing paperwork. You can get a little extra sleep. I used to take the bus to work, and I did all of these. I also met some interesting people.

One was a young woman who worked for a financial institution. We sat together from time to time, and she was good company. She made me laugh.

One winter Saturday back in the 1970s, at about six o'clock in the morning, I was awakened by the persistent ring of the doorbell. I looked outside, saw it was snowing heavily, walked down the stairs, and opened the front door. Standing there was my friend from the bus, covered with snow and visibly frightened.

She came in, I took her coat, and she sat down at the dining room table.

"My husband is trying to kill me," she said.

"What would you like me to do?" I asked.

"I want to live here with you and your family," she told me. "I'll be safe here."

At this point, my wife came down and we offered her tea. "I'm sorry," I said, "but you can't live here. We don't have a spare room."

"If I can't live here," she responded, "then I'll go to the FBI, and they will help me get a new identity."

"That isn't going to work either," I told her, "and the FBI isn't open on Saturday."

I suggested we go to the local hospital. She said no, hesitated for just a moment, and came up with another idea.

"I'm Jewish," she said. "I'll go to Israel, where I will be safe."

I pointed out the difficult logistics of such a move and asked, "What about the Beth Israel? You'll be safe there."

She knew I was referring to a Boston hospital, but the fact that it had "Israel" in the name appeased her, and she agreed.

And that is how we ended up in my car, heading into Boston on unplowed streets. She ducked down so that no one, especially her husband, would see her.

"Are you scared?" she asked.

I admitted that I was, what with the driving snow and an unpredictable passenger who might bolt at any minute. What would I do then?

"I'm scared too," she admitted.

We got to the hospital, and a young psychiatrist took the matter in hand. She eyed me somewhat suspiciously and asked me to wait outside the room. A few minutes later, the doctor came out and told me I had done the right thing. She invited me to come in; my friend wanted me there.

The doctor stepped out briefly, and my young friend asked, "Can I write you a note?"

I nodded yes.

She took a pen from her purse and wrote, "Will you save my husband?"

I told her I didn't know how to save anybody but that she was safe and should let the doctor help her. The hospital admitted her that day.

Soon she was transferred to a longer-term care facility, and over the following weeks she called me several times. She seemed more composed, and I hoped she was getting better. I wished her well, and finally the calls stopped.

Time passed, and I did not see her on the bus. Then, on another Saturday morning a year or so later, the doorbell rang once again. There she was, my friend from the bus.

"How nice to see you," I said. "You look wonderful."

"I have a surprise for you in the car," she replied. She returned a minute later, carrying her new baby boy.

My Elevator Ride and Valentine's Day Hearts

February is a month short on days but long on holidays—Groundhog's Day, Valentine's Day, Presidents' Day, and every four years, Leap Day.

In 2012, February also included a Jewish holiday called *Tu B'Shevat*, which was used in ancient times to determine when the fruit of trees became *kosher* (fit to be eaten). In modern times it marks a day for planting trees in Israel, the Jewish equivalent of Arbor Day. I remember my father telling me, around the time the State of Israel was established in 1948, that we should plant trees there.

That February, I went to visit a friend who had had some health setbacks. He and his wife were living temporarily in a downtown Boston apartment building. I stepped into an elevator that refused to move, so I switched to another and made my way to the thirty-eighth floor.

My friend and I had a good visit.. I left and pushed the down button. The elevator arrived carrying two people, a man and woman.

Breaking the usual elevator silence, I said, "This is my first time in this building." I have no idea why I thought that information would be of any interest to two total strangers.

The woman replied, "It's nice here. People are very friendly."

As we slowly descended, we continued to talk, just casual conversation. I assumed they were from out of town.

"Where are you from?" I asked.

"Upstate New York," the man answered. "We're just living in Boston temporarily."

"We don't know how long we will be here," the woman told me.

The man explained, "My sons are getting new hearts."

As we stepped into the building lobby, I wanted to know more. "Where are they?" I asked. "How old are they?"

The father told me that the two boys, ages eighteen and fifteen, were at Children's Hospital. The older one was a soccer player, he went on, and already had his new heart. The younger one was waiting for his. The father added, "It's a congenital problem."

I thought to myself, "This is really something." I just stepped into an elevator, made a passing comment, and here I am in the middle of a once-in-a-lifetime conversation.

"How are you holding up?" I asked.

The woman replied. "We're doing OK. He's the father, I'm the stepmom."

After wishing them well, I left the husband and wife to return to my office a few blocks away. I couldn't get them out of my mind, and I decided to observe *Tu B'Shevat* the following week, something I'd never done before, by planting two trees in Israel in honor of the boys. You can have them planted in different forests. I picked the Children's Forest.

According to the United States Greeting Card Association, approximately 190 million valentines are sent every year, and that doesn't include e-valentines. Make that one more. The heart is the symbol of the holiday, and even though I didn't know the boys' names, this piece is my valentine to them.

My Freshman Year and the Unorthodox Roommate

"Who knows what evil lurks in the hearts of men? The Shadow knows!"
Introduction to "The Shadow" radio program, 1937–1954

When I was a kid, I listened to radio mystery programs on Sunday afternoons. One character who impressed me then, and has stayed with me ever since, was the "wealthy young man about town" named Lamont Cranston. Like Clark Kent (*Superman*), he had another identity. He was *The Shadow*, a crime-fighter who had the "mysterious power to cloud men's minds, so that they could not see him."

The day I got into college, my sister and I left Claremont for summer camp jobs in upstate New York. When we returned home in late August, my sister, a recent Syracuse University graduate, told me, "You need the right clothes."

We drove downtown to Heller's clothing store on Pleasant Street. An hour later, we left, with me properly outfitted—khaki pants, button-down shirts, cardigan sweaters, penny loafers. Sam Heller had everything I needed.

When my parents and I arrived at my freshman dormitory, my roommate wasn't in the room, but his clothes were hanging in a walk-in closet that we would share—baggy jeans, plaid woolen shirts, old-fashioned black shoes. Not "Ivy League." Not even close.

After a while, Wilson Brown returned to the room, we shook hands, and that was the beginning of our year together. No two people could have been less alike. He had no interest in baseball. He was tall, gangly, stoop-shouldered, wore horn-rimmed glasses, and looked like he needed a shave. When he spoke, he seemed to mumble, an "aw, shucks" kind of guy.

That's the luck of the draw, I must have thought to myself. My good luck, as it turned out.

Over the next nine months, I learned a lot from my roommate. The first lesson I remember had to do with the nameplates on the door to our room. I dutifully wrote my name on a piece of paper and slipped it into the slot. Everyone else did the same, but not my non-conformist

Roommates, Brown University Class of 1961 Freshman Handbook

roommate. He wrote down the name "Lamont Cranston" and put that in his slot on the door. My very own Shadow!

Wilson was neither wealthy nor a man about town, but he quickly became known throughout the Brown University campus as "the Shad." His singular act had made it clear that my roommate had a sense of humor and didn't take himself too seriously.

It didn't take long for me to recognize his other good qualities. He was very smart. He was intellectually way ahead of me, but self-effacing to a fault. And he had wisdom beyond his years. When I got back to school after Christmas and told him my father had died, he instinctively knew how to respond.

Wilson did very well in school, went on to earn a PhD, and became a professor of economics at the University of Winnipeg. He retired a few years ago, but his student evaluations are still online. One student wrote, "He is the best teacher I ever had . . . . He is next to God!"

I'm not sure I would go that far, but my appreciation of him has only increased over the years. Unlike the "real" Shadow, Wilson could not make himself *invisible*. Both his personality and his appearance, including the plaid shirts and baggy pants, made him highly visible, one of a kind. However, he did manage to be *inscrutable*. That fall he posted a sign in our room that said, "Promptness is the Price of Piety."

I still haven't figured out what that means.

The Shadow

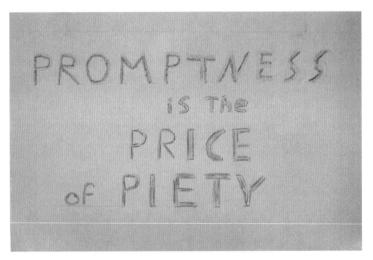

Wilson Brown's sign

My Daughter-in-Law's Relative and the Boston Christmas Tree

I never met Abraham C. ("Cap") Ratshesky, who died in 1943. But we do have two things in common. One of them is that he lived in Boston, and so do I. I'll get around to the second thing later.

Mr. Ratshesky led a full, interesting, and worthwhile life. Before he was forty he had co-founded a bank with his brother, served as a Massachusetts state senator, and attended several national Republican conventions as a delegate.

In addition to politics, charity ran deep in this man. He donated a building to the Red Cross for its headquarters, was a founder of Beth Israel Hospital, and in 1925 helped organize the "Pennies Campaign," a fundraising effort to restore the USS *Constitution*.

In 1916 he created the A.C. Ratshesky Foundation, dedicated to good works, and in World War I he held a public position as Assistant Food Administrator for Massachusetts. In 1930, President Hoover appointed him as United States Minister to Czechoslovakia (his official title was "Envoy Extraordinary and Minister Plenipotentiary").

But the good deed that always comes to mind at this time of the year goes back to December 6, 1917. On that date a French cargo ship, the Mont-Blanc, collided with a Norwegian ship in Halifax Harbour in Nova Scotia. The French ship was full of wartime explosives, and the collision set off the biggest man-made explosion up to that time. Over 2,000 people were killed, thousands were injured, and the city was virtually destroyed.

That very day Mr. Ratshesky sprang into action. At 5:30 p.m., Massachusetts Governor McCall appointed him "Commissioner-in-Charge" of the Halifax Relief Expedition and directed him to "go the limit." The Governor's letter to the mayor of Halifax, dated December 6, 1917, begins, "I am sending Hon. A.C. Ratshesky . . . immediately to your city, with a corps of our best State surgeons and nurses, in the belief that they may be of service to you in this hour of need." The letter concludes, "The Commonwealth of Massachusetts will stand back of

A.C. ("Cap") Ratshesky

Mr. Ratshesky in every way."

"Cap" helped load supplies on the train in Boston, and at 10:00 p.m., he and thirty doctors, nurses, and Red Cross representatives climbed aboard. The next morning they arrived in McAdam Junction, New Brunswick, where they learned that all telegraph and telephone wires in Halifax were down, so no one knew they were coming. The remainder of their trip to Halifax was delayed by a blizzard, and they arrived in the early morning hours of December 8th. Mr. Ratshesky later reported that "the Massachusetts relief train was the first to enter the devastated city."

The next year, as a token of their gratitude, the citizens of Halifax sent a Christmas tree to the City of Boston. Then, more than fifty years later, they turned that single gift into a tradition. Every year for the last forty-two years they have provided the city with its "official" Christmas tree.

When the tree left Halifax in November of 2013, it was led by a group of marathon runners to honor the victims of the Boston Marathon Day bombings. It arrived on December 5th, a 47-foot-tall white spruce. The next day, Mayor Thomas Menino led his last Christmas tree lighting ceremony as mayor, and the tree from Nova Scotia shone again over the Boston Common.

Mr. Ratshesky's spirit lives on, not only in the hearts of Nova Scotia's citizens but in the foundation that bears his name, now nearly one hundred years old. It lives on in my daughter-in-law, Rebecca, as well. Mr. Ratshesky was her great-great uncle, making her the other thing I have in common with this remarkable man.

My Hero Victor and Promises to His Mother

I don't usually write about lawyers, but Victor Garo isn't your usual lawyer. Victor is a sole practitioner with a second-floor walk-up office in Medford Square. When he passed the bar in 1965, his parents took him to lunch.

"Victor," his mother said, "Your father and I are very proud of you. We know you'll be able to make a good living. But promise me one thing—that you will remember your job is to help people."

"I promise," he told her.

A year or so later, a man named Joe Salvati was convicted, along with five others, of participating in the murder of a smalltime thug named Teddy Deegan. The judge sentenced him to life without the possibility of parole.

A decade later, in 1977, a client of Victor's called from prison and told him that a man named Joe Salvati needed a lawyer. Victor went to see him, and Salvati claimed he was innocent. Victor had heard that story before but agreed to look at the court file and talk to some people.

The only witness against Salvati at trial was a professional hit-man named Joe "The Animal" Barboza, who testified that the Mafia had hired him to kill Deegan and that he had recruited Salvati to drive the getaway car. The jury believed his testimony, but Victor wasn't so sure. After reading the trial transcript, he thought to himself, "This just doesn't add up."

He went back to see Salvati and agreed to see if he could reopen the case.

"How much will it cost?" Salvati asked.

"I'd like a $1,500 retainer," Victor answered.

Marie Salvati brought the $1,500 to Victor's office. He later learned she had borrowed the money, and that she and the four Salvati children were barely getting by. Victor gave back the money.

"She needed it more than I did," Victor told me a long time later.

Over the next ten years, Victor spent countless hours on what everyone told him was a hopeless case. No fee, but a strong belief in his client's innocence. He did research, filed motions, knocked on doors, met with the Parole Board, all to no avail.

Victor Garo

During that time, Victor lived with his parents in Medford. Salvati often called the Garo home during the evening, using a prison payphone. Many times Victor would still be at work, so his mother would talk to Salvati. During those conversations, she got to know him, and through him his wife and his children.

Victor's mother became ill in the late 1980s. One evening, Victor was sitting by his mother's bedside. "Victor," she said, "promise me you will keep trying to help Mr. Salvati."

"I didn't know it meant so much to you," he said.

"It does," she told her son. "I believe he is an innocent man. Without you, he won't have anyone to help him."

"I promise," Victor replied.

Ten more years went by, hundreds—no thousands—of hours of

work, and eventually Victor started to make progress. In 1997, the Parole Board decided that Salvati, a model prisoner, should be released, and the Governor commuted his sentence.

Victor and his client wanted more, and they got it. In 2001, the Massachusetts court overturned Salvati's conviction. Victor proved that Salvati actually *was* innocent, set up by Barboza and corrupt FBI agents who knew that Barboza was lying but chose to protect their "sources." As a result, Joe Salvati missed out on 30 years—his four children growing up, their marriages, grandchildren, christenings, holidays—everything that makes life worthwhile.

Victor had been with him for twenty of those years, keeping his first promise, the one he made to his mother the day he passed the bar. On March 20, 1997, the day he walked Joe Salvati through the doorway from prison to freedom, Victor kept the second promise, the one he made at his mother's bedside. Joe, Marie, their children, and grandchildren didn't go directly home. Their first stop was the cemetery.

Victor took Joe over to his mother's gravestone. "Ma," he said, "I brought you Joe."[9]

---

9 Salvati wasn't Barboza's (and the FBI's) only victim. Three other men were also wrongfully convicted of murdering Deegan, based on Barboza's perjured testimony. All four were ultimately cleared, but two of them died in jail. Their families, along with Salvati and the other survivor, Peter Limone, sued the FBI. In 2007 the federal court awarded damages of $101.7 million. Salvati received the largest share—over $34 million.

DOM DiMAGGIO
outfielder BOSTON RED SOX

Sports

My Lifelong Addiction and Words to Live By

According to the late Bill Veeck, who owned three major league baseball teams, the true harbinger of spring isn't the blooming of crocuses or birds flying north, but the sound of a bat on a ball. Another owner, Walter O'Malley, explained that baseball is more like a disease than a business.

I've been infected with that particular illness most of my life, and I don't want to be cured. Besides, it's a form of patriotism. The poet Walt Whitman called baseball "our game, the American game."

At the beginning of the 2011 season, Red Sox fans asked themselves the usual questions. "Is the team healthy? Will the new players work out? What about the relief pitchers? Can Daisuke Matsuzaka throw strikes?" As usual (albeit with two recent exceptions) we were in "Wait 'til next year" mode, and here it was again, next year.

Answers to those and other questions would have to await the end of the season, and when they came it wasn't pretty. However, every spring we are reminded of why baseball captivates so many of us, the wisdom of its sages. Has any other sport produced such philosophers? I doubt it.

One of my favorite pieces of advice is "Don't look back. Something might be gaining on you." Those words come from Satchel Paige, the ageless pitcher who played in the Negro Leagues most of his career and finally made it to the majors late in the day. He also said, "Avoid running at all times."

We all know about Yogi Berra, who claims "I never said most of the things I said."

Maybe not, but I'm sure glad he said them. Thanks to him, we all know "It ain't over till it's over," but my favorite Yogi advice is "If you come to a fork in the road, take it." A close second is, "You should always go to other people's funerals; otherwise, they won't come to yours."

A. Bartlett Giamatti, the actor Paul's father, went from being a Yale professor to becoming Commissioner of Major League Baseball. He was born in Boston, not far from Fenway Park, so he knew what he was talking about when he said of the game, "It breaks your heart. It is designed to break your heart." 2011 was such a year.

Fortunately, at least when it comes to baseball, broken hearts have short memories.

Baseball is how many of us measure the seasons. Commissioner Giamatti wrote, "It begins in the spring . . . blossoms in the summer . . . and leaves you to face the fall alone."

Hall of Fame infielder Rogers Hornsby once said he spent his winters staring out the window waiting for spring. I remember doing the same thing in Claremont long ago. We usually couldn't wait, so we would oil our gloves and start even before the snow melted. I remember how hard it was to find baseballs in snow banks.

The game of baseball is more than just balls and strikes, hot dogs and statistics. As our Walpole neighbor Ken Burns pointed out in his PBS documentary series *Baseball*, the sport helped Americanize many of those who arrived at Ellis Island starting in 1892. My grandfather was one of those immigrants. I caught the disease from him.

Fenway Park, 2008

My Spring Fancy and a Lasting Disappointment

In the late 1940s, my cousin Carl was the catcher for the Stevens High School baseball team, the Cardinals. I pictured myself as the next "Steinie," which is what they called him. He and Phil Kaminsky were an all-Jewish battery, the only one in the school's history. Phil even got a tryout with the Red Sox. Carl went on to become Dave Sisler's catcher at Princeton, and Sisler became a Red Sox pitcher.

As for me, no one ever called me "Steinie." And I didn't make the Stevens High baseball team. It still hurts.

Early in the 2011 season, I wrote that the Red Sox were "off to a rocky start" but added "it's a long season." Unfortunately, that season turned out to be too long for the Red Sox. On Labor Day it seemed a sure thing they would make the playoffs. Instead, the team fell apart, leaving us muttering the old refrain, "Wait 'til next year."

In the blink of an eye, next year arrived, and this not-so-young man's fancy turned, once again, to thoughts of . . . baseball. Terry Francona was gone, leaving it to the new manager, Bobby Valentine, to pick up the pieces. Heidi Watney was gone too. Now those were tough shoes to fill.

Why do so many of us follow the game of baseball, and feel a bit forlorn from the end of one season to the beginning of the next? Maybe it's because our favorite team gets to start over every spring, and we don't. If our bones ache, or our hearing fails, or our eyes dim, too bad. We're stuck with what we've got. Not so in baseball. The Red Sox can simply cast off the parts that no longer work so well, the Variteks and the Wakefields, and replace them with new blood. I'm glad the team re-signed "Big Papi" Ortiz. At thirty-six and counting, he's practically ancient.

Pitchers and catchers reported to spring training on my birthday this year. The rest of the players arrived a few days later, and the exhibition season got underway. If you happened to be in Fort Myers, you could go to brand-new JetBlue Stadium and buy a box seat ticket for only $46. During the regular season, it costs more than twice that amount at not-so-new Fenway Park. No wonder they call it "Moneyball."

Or you could have gone to Manchester to see the Fisher Cats. Unlike the Red Sox, they were league champions in 2011, and a box seat costs $10. Unfortunately, they're affiliated with the Toronto Blue Jays.

But, if you are serious about our national pastime, there is no experience quite like walking up the ramp at ancient Fenway Park, one hundred years old in 2012, and looking out on that field of green. The usher will show you to your seat and, if it's wet, even wipe it dry. You can put worldly cares out of mind, at least for a few hours. And you can watch the food vendors throw ice creams and peanuts with deadly accuracy and make change on the fly—a show within the Show. You can even have a beer, so long as you don't take it into the clubhouse. That era is over.

There is another choice. This year the Stevens High School team will be in Cheshire County to play both the Conant Orioles and the ConVal Cougars. Like the Red Sox, the Cardinals also had a long season in 2011. They won three games, lost fifteen. If I could, I would try out one last time.[10]

---

10 Bobby Valentine lasted only one season as the Red Sox manager, and the team finished in last place, twenty-six games behind the New York Yankees. Ortiz was out for much of the year, and the Red Sox cleaned house in the fall, trading several high-profile players who hadn't lived up to expectations. John Farrell took over as manager for the 2013 season, and Big Papi returned with a vengeance. The team went from last place to first, won the American League pennant, and went on to win the World Series against St. Louis in six games.

My Hot Corner and the Loss of Innocence

I loved summer camp. I went for three summers when I was nine, ten, and eleven—overnight camp, eight weeks each time. It was on one of the picturesque Belgrade Lakes in Maine.

You'd think my parents would have driven me from Claremont across New Hampshire and then up to Waterville. Or maybe north to North Conway, and then east. That would be a logical assumption, but it would be wrong.

No, my parents drove me *south*, to Boston, and put me on a train at North Station. I have no idea why they did that, and I never thought to ask. Maybe they wanted me to bond with the Boston kids who were on their way to the camp. Or maybe, in those days, it was even harder to go across the state than it is now.

By my first camp season I already loved baseball. My friends and I played it even before the snow fully melted in the spring, and well after the leaves had fallen in the fall. I started out as a third baseman, and I told my parents that I was at the "hot corner," which is how my grandfather always referred to that position. My mother, who knew nothing about baseball and hardly ever bragged about her kids, couldn't resist telling her friends that her son had picked the coolest part of the field. She must have misheard me.

I didn't have a strong throwing arm, and the first baseman, a tall kid from Philadelphia, suggested that I move over to second base. The catcher, my friend Herbie Hodos, agreed.

After that first year at camp, a relative got me a major league baseball autographed by Billy Southworth, manager of the pennant-winning (but World Series-losing) Boston Braves. He inscribed the ball, "To Joey, my next second baseman." Some of the players also signed the ball. One late winter day, my friends and I needed a ball, I foolishly used it, and we managed to lose it in the snowy woods.

Life has its disappointments, and mine is no exception. Even worse than losing that baseball is the fact that I didn't make the high school baseball team. By then the Braves had left Boston, Billy Southworth was no longer managing, and I had started to adjust to the reality that I would have to look for another line of work when I grew up. Still, more than half a century later, I have not fully recovered.

A few years ago, I reconnected with our summer camp catcher, who had gone on to become a judge in Greenfield, Massachusetts. The first thing I asked was about his later baseball career. He was really good when we were campers together, and sure enough, he played in both high school and college—at Yale! He didn't ask, and I didn't mention the fact that my baseball career got cut short. In truth, it never existed.

As for our tall first baseman, I don't know whether he made his high school team, and I haven't seen him since our camp days. But I do know how he turned out. After defending major league criminals as a lawyer, Oscar Goodman became the mayor of Las Vegas.[11]

---

11 About sixty years after my camp days in Maine, I caught up with another member of our baseball team, my camp bunkmate Matt Levine. He lives not far from my daughter in San Francisco. Matt told me that he had recently visited Las Vegas and dropped in on Oscar. They reminisced about camp.

My High School Sports and the Last Basket

In Claremont, we played sports year round when we were kids. My cousin Carl was the Stevens High School varsity quarterback in the late 1940s, and I wanted to follow in his steps.

I tried out for junior varsity football and made the team, but I think everyone did. And, even though I had a weak arm, I became the starting quarterback. I threw the occasional incomplete pass, but mostly my role was to hand off the ball and get out of the way. That was fine with me, since practically everyone was bigger than I was.

I didn't love practice. We would line up for scrimmage, and some of my lineman friends thought it was a good idea to "brush block," meaning to let the defense plunge right through and aim for me. Mostly I was able to get away, but not always.

One time I got hit, went down, and my elbow struck the ground. It was quite a jolt, and for some reason my fingers started to curl.

"My hand, my hand," I cried out.

"Run it off, Steinfield," the coach said.

We didn't have a very successful season—zero wins, eight losses—so I gave up football.

Basketball was another sport we all played, starting in grade school. I hoped for the nickname "Cooz," after the Boston Celtics star Bob Cousy. No one ever called me that, but I did make the junior varsity, coached by the same junior high school teacher who showed no sympathy for my curled fingers.

My playing time was mostly in practice. During games, I sat on the bench at the far end from the coach, waiting for him to call my name. That usually happened when we were way ahead or way behind. "Garbage time," it's called.

I did get into a game my sophomore year, and I remember every second. I would say every minute, but I'm not sure I was on the court for a full minute.

Right after I entered the game, a member of the other team went to the foul line. I was in the backcourt. He missed, our center got the rebound, I ran, and the ball came flying my way. I caught it and started towards the basket, hoping for an easy layup.

STEVENS JAYVEE basketball squad for 1954. Front row left to right, Charles Johnson, Dolek Pilot, Joe Maiola, coach; Bernard Fairbanks and Rodney Brock. Second row, left to right, Skip Nolin, Charles Michalenoick, Dominick Zotto, Don Fletcher, Peter Gauthier and Joseph Steinfield.

Daily Eagle Photo—Titchen

The problem was that someone was in my way, so I did what I had to do. After all, I wasn't getting my hands on the ball very often. I stopped fifteen feet or so from the basket, jumped and shot—left-handed! *Swish*— my "Cooz" moment, and I was fouled in the act of shooting.

I made the foul shot for my first, and as it turned out my last, three-point play. I can still hear the sound as the cheerleaders called my name.

Unfortunately, so did Coach "Run-It-Off." "Steinfield!" he yelled. "You're out!"

Later he told me, "You had no business taking that shot." The fact that I had made the basket and the foul shot apparently didn't count, although nobody told the scorekeeper, and it showed up the next day in the *Daily Eagle* box score.

And that marked the end of my basketball career. I spent the rest of the season on the bench, but it was worth it. [12]

---

12 Much later in life, I had a second "Cooz" moment. I was the junior lawyer in a case representing several Worcester businessmen. They came to our office one day, and I walked into the conference room. One of them came over, extended his hand, and said, "I'm Bob Cousy." "Bob," I replied, "I know who you are."

My Cousin's Bar Mitzvah and Dominic DiMaggio

In 1954, my parents and I drove from Claremont to Boston to attend my cousin Jeff Epstein's *bar mitzvah*. I sat in the back seat, complaining much of the way about how long it was taking to get there. As usual, we got lost once or twice. This was long before Routes 89 and 93, and even longer before GPS.

I was still mourning the departure of the Braves from Boston the previous year, but my lifelong addiction to the Red Sox had begun. What a nuisance to have to drive such a distance, get dressed up, and miss listening to Saturday's game.

We stayed at a hotel and went to the ceremony in Dorchester the next morning. I knew that my cousin's father was friendly with baseball players. He was the one who got me the ball autographed by the Braves manager, the one I lost in the snow. What I didn't know was that "The Little Professor," Dominic DiMaggio, was now in business with my cousin's uncle on his mother's side. He had retired as the Red Sox center fielder at about the same time the Braves left town.

Dom was one of my heroes. We used to sing, "Who's better than his brother Joe? Dominic DiMaggio." I don't remember seeing him at the synagogue.

But I do remember seeing him at the Copley Plaza Hotel luncheon that followed. Not only were he and his wife Emily there, but they were seated at *my* table! Or perhaps we were seated at *his*. Any longings to be in Claremont immediately vanished.

I have no memory of what they served for lunch, or what the adults talked about, but I do recall one thing: I asked Mr. DiMaggio a question.

Just imagine—a fourteen-year-old boy meeting Dom DiMaggio and actually being able to speak with him. Did I ask him about what it was like to be a big league player, playing alongside Ted Williams? Or about Birdie Tebbetts, the catcher from New Hampshire? Or about the unfortunate 1948 season, still fresh in my memory, when Cleveland won the playoff game against the Red Sox for the pennant? Or about the equally unhappy 1949 outcome, when the Yankees won on the last day of the season?

No, I did not ask about any of that. My question, the question any fourteen-year-old boy from New Hampshire would naturally ask, was, *"Have you met her?"* The "her," of course, was Marilyn Monroe, Dom's brother Joe's new wife.

I remember the answer. "Not yet. Next week. We're going down to New York."

That is the closest I ever got to Marilyn Monroe. But I did meet up with Dom and Emily DiMaggio a few years ago, at a charitable event in Boston. I walked over to them and said I wanted to re-introduce myself. I then told them we had sat together at my cousin's *bar mitzvah*, more than fifty years before.

Dom looked me in the eye and said, "Joe, you haven't changed a bit!"

"Neither have you," I answered, thinking to myself, "I'll bet he could still play center field."

When I gave my cousin's name, they remembered being at the luncheon. I asked whether they remembered the question I had asked. No, they admitted they didn't. So, I refreshed their memories: "Have you met her?"

Emily DiMaggio looked at me and said, "Oh," followed by a long pause, and then . . . *"Marilyn."*

My Visit to Fenway and a Tip of the Hat

A few years ago, I happened to be in South Dakota, and I made a new friend in Rapid City. He took me to see two nearby sculptures. One was Mount Rushmore, a tribute to four presidents. The other was the Crazy Horse Memorial, which has been under construction since 1948. It is more than half finished, and worth a trip to South Dakota. I spent a day with members of the Lakota tribe at the Rosebud Reservation in a town named Mission.

My new friend told me he had never visited New England. I told him we used to have the Old Man of the Mountain, but he is no more, and the Presidential Range doesn't have any stone faces. I urged him to come anyway and said I would think of something we could do together.

He called me in April of 2012. He and his two grown sons were planning a trip to Boston and did I have any suggestions.

"Do you like baseball?" I asked.

"We sure do," he answered.

And so the four of us spent a perfect Sunday afternoon at Fenway Park, watching the Red Sox beat the Atlanta Braves. So far as I know the Braves, despite their name, have no connection to American Indians. And Red Sox outfielder Jacoby Ellsbury, who is Navajo on his mother's side, was out with an injury.

My friend told me not to worry. South Dakota has no shortage of Native American culture, but it is deficient when it comes to baseball. They have the Sioux Falls Pheasants (formerly called the "Canaries"), but those birds aren't even affiliated with a major league team.

We met at Fenway Park and, as luck would have it, they're Red Sox fans. David Ortiz had the day off, but Kevin Youkilis, the other remaining member of the 2004 championship team, was in the lineup. There he was at third base, practically right in front of us.

He played flawlessly in the field, then came up in the seventh inning with the Sox ahead and a man on base. "Youk, Youk!" the fans cried. We all knew that this was probably his last at-bat as a member of the team. He was 33 and, unlike Ortiz who is even older, not having a very good

Chief Crazy Horse and me in 2005

year. Will Middlebrooks, ten years younger, was taking over at third.

The pitch came in—I don't know what it was. A fast ball? A curve? A slider? A cutter? Whatever it was, he hit it hard and straight and true, on a line to left centerfield. Two outfielders converged, but neither one caught it. The baseball gods were smiling as Youk steamed from second to third, straight at us. The throw flew from the outfielder to the cutoff man, and from him to the third baseman. The ball and the runner arrived together, but Youk slid under the tag, safe. A triple.

In came a pinch-runner, and Youkilis headed for the dugout. Before he got there, teammates came onto the field, jostling for a chance to hug their soon-to-be-gone teammate. Youkilis doffed his cap—what other sport pays so much attention to that simple act?—then disappeared from view. The four of us, and everyone else in the park, kept shouting "Youk!" and he came out for a cap-tipping encore. Then he was gone, about to undergo a simple change of apparel, from red sox to white, to play baseball a lot closer to South Dakota.

Like Ted Williams, who never tipped his cap, Youkilis is known for getting a lot of bases on balls. The book *Moneyball* gave him a nickname, "the Greek god of walks." His ancestors moved from Romania to Greece a long time ago, but they didn't stay long, and their name wasn't originally Youkilis. It was Weiner.

My grandson Jacob called me up after the trade. "Grandpa," he said, "now the Red Sox don't have any Jewish players."

My Favorite Sport and the Passage of Time

In December, the season is over, and I can put my glove away for a few months.

Our New Hampshire poet, Donald Hall, told Ken Burns, "Baseball . . . is a place where memory gathers." I wish I'd said that.

Baseball is the great equalizer. You can talk about it with the man at the dry cleaners, the cab driver, the young immigrant working at the convenience store, your grandchildren. What is it about baseball that fascinates? Maybe it's because the games last as long as they last, unlike other team sports that have a fixed time limit. Maybe it's the endlessness of statistics seeking to measure quality and success. Or maybe, for some of us, it's still a field of dreams we once had.

Larry Tye's book, *Satchel,* is a biography of the famous pitcher, but it is also a tribute to the old Negro Leagues, where Satchel Paige began pitching in the 1920s. If you haven't read it, do yourself a favor and go to your nearest bookstore or library. You'll see what Ken Burns meant when he called baseball "the story of America."

When I was six or seven, my grandfather sat me down one day and began to explain. "Joey," he said, "there are two leagues, the American and the National."

A year or two later, Satchel Paige, who by then was probably closer to fifty than to forty years old, became the oldest big league rookie ever. (My grandfather loved that word, "rookie"—which he said with a Yiddish accent.) Satchel even pitched briefly in the 1948 World Series, the one where the Indians beat the Boston Braves, who skulked out of town a few years later, never to return.

We would leave Claremont early in the morning, my grandfather and I, get lost at least once on our way to Boston, and still arrive at Fenway Park in time for batting practice. "Look, Joey," my grandfather would say. "There's Ted Williams."

Roger Kahn's *The Boys of Summer* is another priceless baseball book. He has written about sports for a long time, but his 1972 tribute to the Brooklyn Dodgers is in a class by itself. It is much more than a book about baseball. It tells the stories, some heartbreaking, of players such as Pee Wee Reese, Duke Snider, Carl Furillo, and others who played at the crossroads of baseball and life in America—the arrival in 1947 of Jackie Robinson, the first black person to play in the major leagues.

Those athletes are now memories, and while many of today's players are cut from their mold (New York's Derek Jeter and Boston's Dustin Pedroia come to mind), many are not. Performance-enhancing drugs have polluted the pastime, with talk of placing asterisks next to record holders such as Barry Bonds.

I'm not saying the old-timers were so perfect. Babe Ruth was a serious drinker, Ty Cobb according to most accounts was an awful person, and racism was present on the field in 1947. Still, times have changed since my grandfather's day, and it's hard to look up to players the way we once did.

Paul Simon seems to have anticipated the problem in his memorable lyrics for the movie *The Graduate*. "Where have you gone Joe DiMaggio? Our nation turns its lonely eyes to you."

The last line of the song answers the question. "What's that you say, Mrs. Robinson? Joltin' Joe has left and gone away."

Even so, of one thing we can be sure. The snow will melt in the spring, and it will be time to take out the glove for the new season. Do they still use neat's foot oil?

NEWPORT
JAZZ
FESTIVAL

Second Annual
Newport Jazz Festival

DIRECTED BY GEORGE WEIN

Friday
Evening
Program
8:30 PM

Louis Armstrong All Stars
Roy Eldridge
Erroll Garner Trio
Coleman Hawkins
Woody Herman
Teddi King
Stan Rubin's Tigertown Five
Joe Turner
Jo Jones

Saturday
Evening
Program
8:30 PM

Chet Baker
Ruby Braff
Bob Brookmeyer
Dave Brubeck
Al Cohn
Wild Bill Davison
Vic Dickenson
Buzzy Drootin
Milt Hinton

Lee Konitz
Warne Marsh
Marion & Jimmy McPartland
Max Roach-Clifford Brown
Pee Wee Russell
Dinah Washington
George Wein
Bud Freeman

Sunday
Evening
Program
8:30 PM

Count Basie
Dave Brubeck
Duke Ellington
Bobby Hackett
Percy Heath
Jo Jones
Modern Jazz Quartet
Gerry Mulligan
Miles Davis

Thelonius Monk
Bud Shank
Johnny Smith
Billy Taylor
Kai Winding-J. J. Johnson
Ben Webster
Lester Young
Jimmy Rushing

Forums at
Belcourt,
Bellevue Ave.

Saturday,
3:00 PM

Sunday,
3:00 PM

FREE ADMISSION

OUTSIDE JAZZ — Richard Waterman, anthropologist, Northwestern U.; Dr. Norman Margolis, psychiatrist; Henry Cowell, composer; Willis James, folklorist, Spelman College; Eric Larrabee, editor of Harper's magazine; Father Norman O'Conner, C.S.P., of Boston University as moderator. Concert by Bob Wilbur and The Six.

INSIDE JAZZ — Dave Brubeck, Gerry Mulligan and Billy Taylor representing the musicians, and Wilder Hobson of Newsweek, Nesnui Ertegan of Atlantic Records, Marshall Stearns of Hunter College, Father O'Conner and Gunther Schuller representing the critics. Concert: Charlie Mingus, Teo Macero, Rudy Nichols, Teddy Charles, John LaPorta, Eddie Bert and Art Farmer.

Arts

My Teenage Jazz Festival and Duke Ellington

Somewhere around the age of thirteen, I became interested in jazz music. The modern era of long-playing records was underway, and I soon had a collection that included the great bands and soloists of the era. I wasn't the only kid in Claremont who was interested in jazz, and a few of us would go to weekend jam sessions and hear amateurs who sounded like pros. One of them was Winston Keating (everybody called him "Buster"), my friend Ray's father. He had been a professional drummer but gave it up to raise a family and open an insurance agency. I had a hard time understanding that decision, but he told me he never regretted it. As he explained it, life on the road isn't all it's cracked up to be.

The first Newport Jazz Festival was held in July of 1954. I turned sixteen early the next year and asked my father if I could borrow his car for a few days so that Ray and I could drive to Rhode Island to attend that summer's Festival. He said yes—a trusting man my father—so we and two other guys, Mike and Vic, organized our own road trip.

Off we went that July. What an experience—jazz under the stars three nights in a row, and the best seats at five dollars apiece. All the greats were there—Louis Armstrong, Miles Davis who played his historic "Round Midnight" with Thelonious Monk on piano, Dave Brubeck, Gerry Mulligan, Ella Fitzgerald—and the big bands of Woody Herman, Count Basie, and Duke Ellington. If I could keep reliving those three nights in Newport, Rhode Island, sort of a musical version of the movie *Groundhog Day*, I would gladly do so.

More than 50 years have passed, my musical tastes have changed somewhat, but no concert I have attended has equaled the pure pleasure of the music we heard that summer. You can buy the original program book on eBay for about sixty dollars. I think I'll settle for my one-page list of the musicians, which tells you all you need to know.

When I was in college, a few years later, I met Duke Ellington. That experience, too, has stayed with me. In fact, it has become indelible—literally.

The Ellington band was performing at a jazz club in Boston called Storyville, named after a section of New Orleans known for jazz and less savory activities. They agreed to perform a "runout" concert at our Rhode

Island campus, and a friend of mine was in charge of the event. He knew I liked jazz and asked if I would like to go to Boston and show some of the musicians how to find the gymnasium where the concert was being held.

A few days later I took the train to Boston, found my way to Storyville, and there he was—Duke Ellington. "Let's go," said his driver Mo, and we got into the Duke's robin's egg blue Cadillac, Mr. Ellington and Mo in the front, saxophone player Paul Gonsalves and his wife and me in the back.

At that moment, sitting behind his driver and watching Duke Ellington wrap band-aids around his fingers, I thought I was living a dream. Then things started not to go so well, and soon they became nightmarish. I was the guide, and we left with enough time to arrive by two o'clock. I thought I knew how to get there, but there was no Interstate 95 in those days, no GPS device to help you out, and it turned out that even in the small state of Rhode Island you could get hopelessly lost. Which is what we did. Mr. Ellington was not pleased.

Decades later, I was at a concert in Boston and told this story to an acquaintance. It had taken that long before I could tell anyone about this particular mishap. I didn't realize it at the time, but my acquaintance was also a jazz fan, and a collector of books on the subject. The next day, he sent me a page from a book called "Duke Ellington Day by Day." That book contains a chronology of every concert Ellington ever performed. Unfortunately, the author didn't leave out a certain concert in Rhode Island, and there it is in black and white:

> "March 14, 1959—this afternoon concert . . . was scheduled to start by 2p.m. When Ellington did not show up on time, a quartet . . . began to entertain the waiting crowd at 2:30 and played for an hour before Ellington and Paul Gonsalves completed the sextet for the remainder of the program."

I am grateful to the author of the book for reducing the delay by at least thirty minutes, and even more so for not mentioning me.[13]

---

13 Gonsalves fell asleep on our way to Rhode Island, and when he woke up we were somewhere near Olneyville. "Where are we?" he asked. "Lost," said Mo. "Hell," Gonsalves replied, "why didn't you wake me up? I'm from Pawtucket."

My Rock Star and Ozzy Osbourne's Conditions

Long before he became a television reality show personality, Ozzy Osbourne was just a regular rock star. One time, he was on tour and booked to play the Boston Garden. Someone reported to the Licensing Commission that Ozzy abused animals. According to the story, he had bitten off the head of a chicken while onstage, and Boston's rock radio stations interrupted whatever they were playing with an urgent bulletin: The license to perform had been revoked, the concert was off.

That's where I came in. The band was on its way north from Hershey, Pennsylvania, and their New York lawyer somehow found me and asked if I could do something about this unfortunate turn of events. I asked, "Who is Ozzy Osbourne?"

Despite my woeful ignorance of rock music, I found myself representing Ozzy before the Licensing Board on a Wednesday. Perhaps fearing a ticketholder riot, the Board reinstated the license but imposed several strict conditions: *No obscenity. No nudity. No pyrotechnics. No violence. No feigned violence.*

I called the New York lawyer and gave him a full report. I asked him to pass these details on to the band, and he promised he would. He suggested that I call the backstage number on the day of the concert and speak with Sharon, Ozzy's manager. (Yes, the same Sharon you've seen on television, but this was before they were married.)

Late Friday afternoon, I called the backstage number and let it ring about twenty times. Someone finally answered, and I asked if I could please speak with Mr. Osbourne. "They've gone out to eat," he said. I left a message and my telephone number, not really expecting a return call.

I was wrong. Within an hour, Sharon called me back and invited me to come over. She gave me directions to get backstage, and off I went, probably the only person who ever went to a rock concert wearing a suit and tie.

When I found my way through the special entrance Sharon told me to use, there they were, Ozzy Osbourne and the members of his band. Sharon introduced herself and took me to meet the great man. We chatted for a few minutes while he painted one side of his face one color and the other side a different color. He swore he had never bitten the head off a chicken and told me the real story of how that rumor got started.

Ozzy Osbourne told me that as a boy in England, he had worked as an assistant in a slaughterhouse, so he knew quite a lot about animals. One time when he was performing, a fan threw something on stage. Ozzy picked it up and bit it, thinking it was a stuffed animal. It turned out to be a dead bat. "I know that you don't bite a dead animal," he told me, "and I paid the price. I had to have a series of rabies shots, and they were damned painful."

Then he asked if I would like to meet the members of the band. I said I would, and Sharon walked me over and made the introductions. I told them who I was and asked if they knew about the licensing problem. No one did.

"Well," I explained, "this is Boston." "We know that," said the lead guitar player, who served as the group's spokesman.

"Do you know about the conditions?" I asked. The question drew blank looks, followed by, "What conditions?"

Thanks a lot, my New-York-lawyer-friend, I thought. So I explained them, one by one:

"No obscenity."

"No problem," the guitar player said.

"No nudity."

"No problem."

"No pyrotechnics."

"No problem."

"No violence."

"No problem."

"No feigned violence."

This time, no response.

I repeated, "No feigned violence."

Still no response.

"Is there a problem?" I asked.

The guitarist answered, "Oh, shit. Now we can't hang the midget."

At that point, another member of the band, a midget named Ronnie, looked up and said, "That's OK, you can hang me twice in Hartford tomorrow."

My Love of Theatre and the Play I Missed

My mother loved the theatre, and she saw to it that I did too. It began when I was nine. We drove from Claremont to Boston and saw two plays. One was *Miss Liberty*, a musical starring Eddie Albert, and the other was *Mr. Roberts*, a drama starring John Forsythe.

The only thing I remember about either play is that *Mr. Roberts* was about sailors on a ship during World War II, and there was quite a bit of swearing on stage. I considered trying out a few of those words when we got home, but knowing my mother I thought better of it.

In 1952, we went to New York, and I saw my first Broadway show, *The King and I*. Gertrude Lawrence played Anna, the widow who became the teacher in the royal household. She won that year's Tony award for Best Actress. Yul Brynner played the King of Siam, the role he inhabited for a lifetime. Every time I think of that play, my mind starts humming, *"Whenever I feel afraid, I hold my head erect, And whistle a happy tune, So no one will suspect I'm afraid."*

A few years later, we took another trip to New York and made plans to attend another play. My mother said I could invite my friend Mike, who would be visiting his grandmother in Brooklyn at the same time, and we could pick the show. We chose *Will Success Spoil Rock Hunter?* starring Jayne Mansfield—an easy choice for two sixteen-year-old boys. If you don't know what she looked like, check online or ask an older person. I don't remember anything about the show, but I remember her. She wasn't that year's "Best Actress," not even close, but Mike and I got my parents' money's worth, and I think my father did too.

Before the play, my parents took us to dinner at Danny's Hideaway on East 45th Street. It was a very good restaurant, known for the fact that its menu did not include any prices. After we ate, my father went to get our coats, and we saw him bump into a short black man. When he got back to the table, Mike said, "Mr. Steinfield, do you know who just bumped into?"

"No," my father said.

"That was Sammy Davis, Jr.," Mike told him.

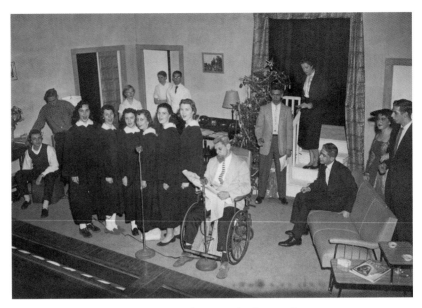

Senior Play, 1957, *The Man Who Came to Dinner*

"Who's Sammy Davis, Jr.?" my father asked.

Mike now lives in Vermont, and we recently met in Claremont for dinner. We reminisced, and he told me that there was a sequel to our evening on Broadway. His initiation into a fraternity at Columbia University included a scavenger hunt. Among the items on his list was "Jayne Mansfield's bra." She was still appearing on Broadway, so off he went to the stage door. Amazingly, he ended up in her dressing room, and she gave him one of her bras.

Then she took it back. "Let me autograph it for you," she said.

As he left, signed bra in hand, Mike told her that he had seen the play two years before and would never forget it. He never has, and neither have I.

Mike and I were in our Stevens High School senior class production of *The Man Who Came to Dinner*. He played Sheridan Whiteside, "the Man," and I played the doctor, a small part. Maybe I wasn't cut out to be on the stage, but being a theatergoer has given me pleasure all my life.

I recently took my grandson to New York for the weekend. I hadn't seen the television show *Glee,* which was being performed live at Radio City Music Hall, but Jacob had. So, assuming it was a play that we would both enjoy, I bought tickets.

It wasn't a play at all, it was a rock concert! I can tell you they haven't changed since I went to see Ozzy Osbourne. Everyone stands up the entire time, they sway back and forth, and the teenagers scream at a decibel level high enough to make bad hearing worse. My grandson had a great time, and I suffered until common sense arrived and I took out my hearing aids.

I missed the musical *Annie* the first time around but would like to see it with my granddaughter, Susie. Dorothy Loudon played Miss Hannigan in the original production, and she *did* win the Best Actress Award for 1977. My mother knew "Dot," as she called her, and my Uncle Eddie went to Stevens High with her. I met her one time. Her mother was my piano teacher.

My Advice for Valentine's Day and the Limits of Social Media

If you think back to the "old days," meaning just a few years ago, you may remember that people used to get together and talk. They still do, but we now have a substitute for human interaction. It's called "social media," where people "get together" online.

Facebook has over a billion subscribers around the world, one for every seven people on the planet. The movie *The Social Network* tells the story of how this phenomenon got started.

A few years ago, I saw a very different sort of movie called *The Station Agent*. I recently saw it again. The movie tells the story of two men and one woman. Finbar, the central character, is played by the actor Peter Dinklage, who is a dwarf. Early in the movie, Finbar, a railroad buff, inherits an abandoned train depot, and he moves into the one-room station.

Is he riveting because of his size? ("Four feet, five inches," he tells a grade-school class while giving a talk about trains.) Yes and no. To be sure, it is hard not to notice the size of a dwarf. As the story develops, however, we see Finbar the person—intelligent, lonely, angry—and his size becomes just one aspect of a complicated human being.

The second principal character is Joey, played by the actor Bobby Cannavale. Each day, he pedals his hot dog stand to the depot, and he tries every way he can to become friends with Finbar. The movie has a lot of great lines, but my favorite is when he asks Finbar, "So, do you people have clubs?"

Finbar glares at him, obviously thinking he is referring to dwarfs. "I mean train clubs," Joey explains.

The third member of the unlikely trio is Olivia, played by Patricia Clarkson. She is a middle-aged woman going through the heartache of losing her young son. "I just looked away for a second," she laments. Wracked with guilt, separated from her husband, she too is alone in the world, trying to cope with life's unfairness.

The Station Agent is my idea of the ultimate anti-social-media movie.

Nobody goes online or sends text messages. Finbar doesn't have a working phone. Joey does but only uses it to talk to his ailing father, in Spanish. Olivia won't answer her phone, since it's her husband calling and there is nothing left to say.

These characters become a community of three. They cry, they get drunk, they laugh, they console.

Today's social media, the critics say, reflect new attitudes towards privacy. According to *Time* magazine, Mark Zuckerberg, creator of Facebook, and Julian Assange, the Wikileaks leaker, "both have a certain disdain for privacy." That's like saying Red Sox fans aren't crazy about the Yankees.

The Station Agent suggests another way of looking at human interaction. Barriers recede and ultimately fall, not by the click of the mouse but by the development of trust. Maybe the critics have it wrong. Maybe the only way we can really relinquish our privacy is by being *with* another person, and allowing him or her to see, to hear, and to touch.

If you only have time for one movie, I recommend *The Station Agent.* As for Valentine's Day this year, I suggest you get together with someone you care about or, if that's not possible, send flowers or a handwritten note. Whatever you do, if you really want someone to be your valentine, don't ask them on Facebook.

My Favorite Poet and the Changing Seasons

"April is the cruellest month," according to the first line of T. S. Eliot's poem "The Waste Land." Eliot left America for England as a young man and lived out his life as a British citizen. He dedicated that poem to Ezra Pound, a poet remembered for being a pro-Nazi anti-Semite who was charged with treason and spent many years in a mental institution. Ever since high school, I've liked poetry, but I never understood Pound's poems and gave up trying long ago.

Robert Frost is another matter entirely. He lived for many years in New Hampshire, but that's not why he's my favorite poet. I just like how his poems sound, and how they rhyme.

> *Whose woods these are I think I know.*
> *His house is in the village though . . .*

At sixteen I had no idea what he was talking about, and when I later learned whose house it was, I thought, "Oh, it's *His* house!"

A few summers ago, the Pianist and I saw *This Verse Business* at the Peterborough Players. Gordon Clapp, whom I remember as Detective Medavoy on the television show *NYPD Blue*, became Robert Frost right in front of our eyes. It turns out he had a head start. Clapp grew up in North Conway and read Frost in school, just as I did in Claremont.

I even like the Frost poems that don't rhyme, the long one called "New Hampshire," for example: "She's one of the two best states in the Union . . ." and "She's . . . a most restful state . . .". The only disconcerting part is the last line: "At present I am living in Vermont" (Frost's other "best state").

Like Eliot, Robert Frost was eccentric, although "irascible" is probably a more accurate word. Long before Frank Sinatra sang his most famous song, Frost was doing it "my way." But unlike the song, he did not travel "each and ev'ry highway." Instead, "Two roads diverged in a wood, and I—I took the one less traveled by."

In Eliot's "The Love Song of J. Alfred Prufrock," as the poem's aging speaker looks at the "evening spread out against the sky," he regrets a life half-lived. "I have measured out my life with coffee spoons," he says.

He sees himself as "deferential . . . politic, cautious, and meticulous . . . Almost, at times, the Fool."

Eliot's Mr. Prufrock seems to have given up. "I grow old . . . I grow old . . . I shall wear the bottoms of my trousers rolled."

Not Frost! True, in "After Apple Picking" he says, "I am overtired, Of the great harvest I myself desired."

And his darker side comes through in another poem, "I have been one acquainted with the night . . . I have outwalked the furthest city light." Yet, while he had "a lover's quarrel with the world," he never stopped pushing back.

> *Ah, when to the heart of man,*
> *Was it ever less than a treason*
> *To go with the drift of things,*
> *To yield with a grace to reason,*
> *And bow and accept the end,*
> *Of a love or a season?*

Unlike Frost, Eliot never lived in New Hampshire, but he was not a stranger to the Monadnock region. There's a torn picture in the Eliot family album at Harvard showing him in Dublin in the summer of 1946. If he'd come earlier in the year, he might have realized that the "cruellest" month is actually March.

My Red Record and an Overdue Apology

But don't change a hair for me
Not if you care for me
Stay little Valentine, stay!
Each day is Valentine's day.

"My Funny Valentine"

Richard Rodgers and Lorenz Hart wrote "My Funny Valentine" in 1937 for a Broadway show called *Babes in Arms*. Frank Sinatra, and practically every other singer, has recorded the song, but my favorite is the instrumental version by Paul Desmond. That name may or may not be a familiar one, but he played alto saxophone in the Dave Brubeck Quartet. Brubeck died in December 2012, one day short of ninety-two, outliving the younger Desmond by thirty-five years.

In an earlier essay, I told the story of my trip from Claremont to Rhode Island, with three friends, to attend the 1955 Newport Jazz Festival. We heard the great jazz musicians of that era. My article didn't tell the whole story of our Newport trip, however, probably because I was too embarrassed.

The four of us, Ray, Vic, Mike, and I, were driving around downtown Newport one afternoon when we spotted Brubeck and Desmond. I pulled over to the sidewalk, and Mike rolled down the window and called out, "Hey, Dave!"

Brubeck turned towards us, and Mike yelled, "You stink!"

Brubeck looked at Desmond, then back at us, as if to say "What the . . . ?"

I drove off. As I recall, none of us chastised Mike. We probably thought it was funny, Stevens High School sophomores being sophomoric.

I still have the 33 1/3 rpm long-playing vinyl record *Jazz at the College of the Pacific*, six songs recorded live in 1953 by the Dave Brubeck Quartet. It is one of two ten-inch records that I own (the other is Benny Goodman's *Session for Six*), and the only one that is red in color, like a valentine. Desmond's "My Funny Valentine" isn't on the record, but if you have a few free minutes on Valentine's Day, you can listen to it on YouTube.

In the summer of 2012, Mike drove over from Vermont for our annual dinner at the Common Man restaurant in Claremont. He brought his daughter, a recent college graduate, and we told her the Newport story.

"Who's Dave Brubeck?" she asked. Her father told her.

"Is he still alive?"

"Yes," he replied.

"Well," she told us, "you should apologize." We nodded our agreement.

I've lost track of Vic, but Ray and Mike remain my dear friends. On the day Dave Brubeck's death was reported in the papers, Ray sent me a two-word email. "Sad news."

I forwarded the email to Mike and remembered his daughter's advice last summer. It's too late now, but Dave and Paul, we apologize. To paraphrase the "My Funny Valentine" lyrics, we care for you both, and we're glad you stayed as long as you did.

Ray Keating, me, and Mike Weiner in Claremont, 2013

St. Basil's Cathedral, Moscow

Travels

My Missing Wallet and the Man at the Front Desk

When we go out of the country, I'm in charge of the passports. No one appointed me, I just assumed the job. Perhaps I should reconsider.

We were in Vienna a few years ago, getting ready for the trip home, sorting through stuff, packing, double-checking the flight time. I had helped organize a two-day conference on the subject of *Terrorism, Media and the Law*, and I was feeling pretty good about myself. Then I suddenly realized that my wallet, the one with the passports in it, was nowhere in sight.

"No problem," I said to myself, "I had it earlier, it must be somewhere, I'll find it."

Minutes passed, I started feeling less good about myself, and I broke down and asked the Pianist, "Have you seen my brown wallet?"

"No," she answered, followed by the classic question, "Where was it the last time you saw it?"

If I knew the answer to that question, I thought, *I wouldn't have asked in the first place.* No time to pick a fight, however.

"I had it at breakfast," I said. "It must be in the room." But where?

They say you should keep your passports separate from your money. Good advice. Remind me to take it next time. So, passports, credit cards, money—all gone missing.

The hotel breakfast room? The only place we'd been that morning. Slow elevator, so down five flights, two steps at a time. It wasn't there. Then to the front desk. It wasn't there either. The man at the desk—a very nice man—came up to the room, and we launched a massive search.

"You had it this morning?" he asked.

"Yes."

"In your pocket?"

"Yes."

"Did you brush up against anyone?"

"No."

"And you're sure you had it this morning?"

"Positive."

"It cannot fly," he said.

I agreed.

By now I was living every traveler's nightmare, and I was worried. We were supposed to leave in the afternoon, and I couldn't think of where else to look. Beads of sweat covered my forehead. Meanwhile, the nice man from the front desk and the Pianist systematically turned the room upside down while I, the original Mr. Cool, sat there in a near-catatonic state. One more trip to the breakfast room. It still wasn't there.

Back to the room, now looking where we'd already looked. Maybe it *did* fly away, which it looked like we wouldn't be doing anytime soon.

Then I heard my new three most favorite words: "Here it is," the Pianist cried out in a voice equal parts triumph and relief. It was, as you might have guessed, exactly where I'd left it for safekeeping.

My First Trip to Russia and the News Back Home

Duende is a hard word to define, especially if you don't know Spanish. I first saw it used by a Spanish writer named Federico Garcia Lorca, and then, in the 1960s and '70s, by a Boston newspaper writer named George Frazier. He used the word to describe people with a certain grace or charm, a style that you recognize when you see it even if you don't quite know what the word really means.

My first trip to Russia was in 1973. We arrived in Moscow on October 5, the day before the Jewish holiday of Yom Kippur. Two days later, I saw a headline in *Pravda* and asked our guide what it said.

She didn't want to answer but finally translated it for me. "It says, 'Jews Attack Arabs.'"

"Yesterday?" I asked. "On Yom Kippur? Do you believe that?"

"Do you believe everything in your newspapers?" she replied, with a look that told me all I needed to know.

The Yom Kippur War was just one of several historic events that took place while we were away. A few days later, Spiro Agnew resigned as vice president, and President Nixon appointed Gerald Ford to replace him. Henry Kissinger won the Nobel Peace Prize.

The day before we returned, President Nixon ordered Watergate Prosecutor Archibald Cox not to turn over the secret White House Tapes. When Cox refused to comply with the order, the president directed Attorney General Elliot Richardson to fire him. Richardson refused and then did the honorable thing. He quit. So did his successor, Deputy Attorney General William Ruckelshaus. This immediately became known as the "Saturday Night Massacre." And it changed history, leading to the resignation of Richard Nixon.

All in all, our time away was a busy two weeks, but we knew little of what had happened. I do remember hearing in Leningrad, as it was then called, that America's new vice president had previously been in the car business. Wrong Ford.

We landed at Kennedy Airport on a Sunday and took a cab to LaGuardia for our plane to Boston. I was starved for news.

"We've been away for two weeks," I told the taxi driver. What did we miss?"

"You missed a lot," he said. "The Knicks lost last night, the Islanders stink, the Giants are awful, and the Mets are about to lose the seventh game of the World Series." I told him I was a Red Sox fan.

We were standing at baggage claim in Boston, and there standing next to us, waiting for his bag, was that debonair columnist, George Frazier. I introduced myself as a loyal reader, he asked where we had been, and I told him Russia for two weeks.

"You missed a lot," he said.

"We heard all about it," I replied.

"Do you know about the Saturday Night Massacre?" he asked.

"Oh, yes," I replied. "Our cab driver in New York brought us completely up to date—the Islanders, the Knicks, the Giants, and the Mets."

Mr. Frazier gave me a puzzled look and then, without missing a beat inquired, "Did he tell you that Willie Mays played his last game?"

"No, he didn't mention that," I replied. "Mays really had it, didn't he Mr. Frazier?"

We both knew the word I had in mind. *Duende.*

My Night at the Opera and the Duty Free Shop

In April of 2008, the Pianist and I were planning to spend two weeks in Samara, Russia, a city I'd never heard of. I had volunteered to teach American law to Russian university students as part of a program called "Senior Lawyers Abroad." I'm old enough, alas, to qualify. When I go to the movies and say "senior ticket, please," they don't even card me.

In order to teach in this program, you have to attend an orientation session in Salzburg, Austria. I did that in March, with a stop in Vienna on the way. Now I know nothing about opera, but someone said that's what you should do in Vienna, so we did.

We checked our coats, and the coatroom lady gave me a ticket. We found our seats for what turned out to be an interminable performance of Wagner's *Die Meistersinger von Nürnberg*. We didn't make it to the third act.

At the coatroom, I gave the lady my ticket, and she returned my coat. When I asked for the Pianist's coat, the answer was, "You only have one ticket."

I said, "You only gave me one ticket."

"You should have asked for the second ticket," she said, holding it up for me to see that she still had it. After some further negotiation, I managed to liberate the second coat.

We took the train to Salzburg and stayed at the Leopoldskron palace, which is near where they filmed *The Sound of Music*, which I liked better than *Die Meistersinger*. We wandered through the streets of the old city, where nearly everything is named after Mozart, including the house where he was born. Then it was time to leave, and we waited for the shuttle to pick us up to take us to the Munich airport for our trip home to Boston by way of Zurich. By then I was out of Euros.

But the van didn't come on time, which prompted me to make several phone calls. Finally, a taxi driver showed up unannounced. He told us he would take us to the van, which was somewhere out on the highway.

On the theory that anything would be better than standing outside a castle in cold, rainy weather, we got in the cab and made our way to a

Leopoldskron Palace, Salzburg, 2008

roadside gas station, somewhere in Germany, where a man was waving at us. Yes, the shuttle driver. He came over and apologized, explaining that he had forgotten to check his list of pickups.

Transferring to the van was not easy—backing up a one way ramp, then taking our baggage down a steep incline, and finally joining six unhappy passengers who had been sitting there for quite a while and were looking at their watches. Planes may not leave on time, but they don't wait for latecomers.

The rest of the ride was unpleasant, what with an unhappy group of fellow travelers and a "shortcut" on winding country roads through a snowstorm in cramped seats. Upon arrival, the driver who hadn't checked his list told me he also didn't take credit cards. So, leaving the Pianist and our baggage as collateral, I went into the Munich airport looking for an ATM machine to get Euros, which is the currency of Germany and most other European countries.

I returned with cash in hand, paid the driver, and we made it through check-in and past security. Not that we needed anything, but I can't resist bargains, so off I went to the duty-free shop. Taking my liquid purchases on board, we arrived at the Zurich airport and rode the tram to the departure gate, all the while listening to the recorded sounds of a Swiss yodeler and Swiss cows.

Then came an unhappy surprise. You have to go through security a second time, and you can't take your duty-free purchases if they happen to be liquids.

I wasn't about to give up my hard-won treasures, so back I went to terminal A, which involved several escalators and another tram ride with the yodeling and cows. After numerous inquiries, I followed the signs to "Exit Zurich" and threw myself on the mercy of Swissair baggage personnel.

Unlike my experience with the opera coatroom attendant in Vienna, I found a sympathetic person who took me to a storage room, came up with a styrofoam container, wrapped my precious goods, and gave me a baggage claim. Then a woman from the airline came along and told me that the container wasn't free.

"Ten Swiss francs, please."

"But I don't have any francs," I said. "How about Euros?"

"We're not in the European Union," came the reply, which is how one learns about international finance.

At this point I had gone too far to quit, and I saw a bank not far from where we stood. I swapped the remainder of my recently obtained Euros for Swiss francs, but when I got back the woman was gone, and nobody wanted the money. So there I was, stuck with ten Swiss francs.

Up and down the escalators I went yet again, back on the tram to terminal E listening to the yodeling and mooing, which I now knew by heart, and up the escalator to the departure gate to rejoin the Pianist, who wasn't smiling. Fortunately, we still had enough time to buy two beers—five Swiss francs each!

My Visa Application and Testing for HIV

It turns out that nothing about a trip to Russia is predictable. We had planned to visit Samara, but we changed our plans. Instead, we decided to go to the Republic of Adygheya, in the southwest corner of Russia, another place I'd never heard of. Here is why we changed our plans.

In order to travel to Russia, you not only need a passport but also a visa, which specifies where you are going and on what dates. There are different types of visas, including tourist, business, and student, among others. If you are going on business, your "host" sends you an "invitation." In our case, that meant that the university would send letters to me and the Pianist, who would be meeting with music students and giving a recital. We would then submit the invitations to the nearest Russian consulate, along with completed applications, our passports, and a bank check for $131 each, no personal checks or credit cards accepted.

The invitation letters from Samara arrived in February, but despite my recent Russian adult education classes, I had no idea what they said. They looked official, however, so I quickly assembled our application materials and sent them to New York by overnight delivery. I soon learned that FedEx had done its job, because the next day my phone rang and the message indicator on the phone said "Russian Consulate." As I lifted the receiver, I suspected this wasn't a social call.

The consulate official began by telling me, in a heavy Russian accent, that they had the papers and everything was fine with one of the applications. The Pianist's invitation said she was going to Russia on "business." My invitation was different. It said I was going to Russia to "study."

"That's a mistake," I said. "I'm going there to give lectures to students."

"It says 'study,'" came the woman's businesslike reply.

Thinking of Khrushchev at the United Nations, I waited for the other shoe to drop. "For a student visa," she said, "you need to send us an HIV test."

"Could you please say that again?" I asked.

And she did. "An HIV test."

"But it's a mistake," I said again.

"Maybe so, but I can't help you. Rules are rules."

The invitation contained another mistake. We were booked to arrive in Moscow on April 10th, but our host had us arriving in Russia a day later. I emailed the university to ask for a revised invitation stating the correct purpose of my visit and the right arrival date. The automatic reply told me my contact person was away on holidays.

So I called my doctor's office, told the receptionist that I needed an HIV test, and asked if I could come by early the next morning. After several minutes on hold, he came back on the line and told me the doctor could see me two weeks from the following Wednesday.

"But you don't understand. I just need a lab test."

"Sorry," he said, "but first you have to come in for counseling."

"I don't want counseling, I want a visa," I said.

He put me on hold again, I heard some soothing music in the background, and he finally came back on the line. "It's a rule," he said. "You have to have counseling, and then you take the test."

I thought to myself, *Here we have two bureaucracies trying to one-up each other. At the rate we're going, the Pianist will get a visa in time for our trip, I won't, and she'll have to give the law lectures.*

At about that time, I got a reply email from someone in Samara telling me that it would be "impossible to give the second variant of the invitation if it has already been given." I think that meant that as far as my invitation was concerned, I was going to Samara to study. As for the incorrect date on the invitation, "Don't worry about it," she advised.

I sent an email to my doctor, who took pity on me and arranged for me to come in the next day and get the test. When I got to the lab, I immediately explained why I was there. "I'm trying to get a visa."

"Sir," the technician said, "many people come in for this type of test."

"I know," I said, "but I'm going to Russia to teach, the university made a mistake on the invitation and said I was coming to study, and that's why I'm here."

She gave me one of those "Now I've heard everything" looks.

A few days later I got the lab report ("negative") and sent it to the Russian Consulate. The visas arrived the next week—with the wrong arrival date, of course. If you saw the movie *The Terminal* with Tom Hanks, you can guess what I was thinking—we'd end up as prisoners at an airport.

Just as I was trying to figure all this out, Samara State did send me a "second variant" but not the one I was looking for. Contrary to previous assurances, our room at the "university hotel" did not come with its own bathroom. Either we would "share," or we could stay at a commercial hotel a half hour's walk away, at our own expense.

That was the last straw. We made a decision. *Dasvidaniya*, Samara.

My Muslim Friend and the Jews of Maykop

After considerable effort, we managed to persuade the Russian Consulate to issue a visa, and in November of 2008 we found ourselves in Maykop, Republic of Adygheya. If you've never heard of the place, don't feel bad. Neither had we, or anyone we know. It's a small speck on the map of a very large country, located in the Northern Caucasus region of southwest Russia. Adygheya has a population of about a half million, consisting mostly of Russians and Adyghes. The latter, sometimes called Circassians, are an ancient people who speak their own language that, at least to my ears, sounds like a lot of consonants with an occasional vowel thrown in.

During our visit we became well acquainted with an Adyghe man named Nehad, who was born and raised in Kfar-Kama, one of two Adyghe villages in Israel. After finishing school and serving in the Israeli Army, he lived in Israel, and for many years in the United States. Several years ago, he paid a visit to his ancestors' birthplace, Adygheya, and was so impressed that he took up residence there. When we met Nehad he had lived in Maykop for two years, and had become completely involved in the business and cultural community.

Like most Adyghe people, Nehad is Muslim. He does not drink alcohol or gamble, follows the dietary rules of his faith, and loves Adyghe music and art. He is deeply committed to helping other Adyghe people do as he has done—return to the homeland from such places as Israel, Jordan, Syria, and Turkey. "Making *Aliyah*," as he puts it, using the Hebrew expression that refers to Jews moving to Israel.

The first day I met Nehad, we went off in his car to visit a new Adyghe settlement a few kilometers from Maykop. With us were the "mayor" of the settlement and two brothers from Turkey who, I later learned, were taking advantage of a free land program for Adyghes willing to return to Adygheya.

On the way out of town, we stopped to visit Nehad's friend Gurevich. "My rabbi," Nehad called him. Gurevich greeted me with the Hebrew words *shalom aleichem*, which mean "peace be upon you." I wished him the same, and that pretty much exhausted

Nehad (with tie), Gurevich (checked shirt), the "Mayor" (far right) and the two brothers

his knowledge of Hebrew, and mine as well.

Like Jews everywhere, the Gurevich family came from someplace else. They emigrated from Poland in the 1960s, about two generations after my grandparents and most of the Jews of Claremont left that country. Gurevich and I got along right away. He asked about my family, and I told him about growing up in New Hampshire. He said he had heard of it, but maybe he was just being polite. He showed me pictures of his family, and we discovered that we both like to fish.

After we left, Nehad told me that a year ago Gurevich decided to hold a *seder*, the ritual meal held on the Jewish holiday of Passover. He sent away for *haggadahs*, the special prayer book that describes the Jewish liberation from slavery in Egypt, as recounted in the Book of Exodus. He invited his Jewish neighbors to attend, and also Nehad. Nehad said he wasn't feeling well, but Gurevich gave him a typical Jewish response.

"You can be sick some other time, I want you to come."

Not wanting to disappoint his friend, Nehad accepted the invitation and arrived at Gurevich's house at the appointed time.

Everyone sat down for the meal, Gurevich brought out the prayer books, and he suddenly realized he had a problem. He didn't know how to read Hebrew, and neither did his fellow *lantsmen* (countrymen).

"Can you read this?" Gurevich asked Nehad.

"Of course I can," Nehad replied. "I'm Israeli."

And so the Jews of Maykop had their first *seder*, led by an Adyghe Muslim.

My Trip to Washington and Holiday Greetings

Claremont in 1948—we got our first rabbi, and the State of Israel was born. Until then it had been Palestine, and I remember wondering how come they changed the name.

I've never seriously considered "making *aliyah*," the term for returning to the Land of Zion. Despite their annual Passover incantation, "Next year in Jerusalem," my grandparents regarded this country as their Promised Land, and I guess I feel the same way. I did visit Israel some years ago, however, eager to see the country which, for Jews around the world, represents the tangible embodiment of the post-Holocaust promise, "Never Again."

The most interesting person we met in Israel was a man named Albert Agazarian. He was the head of public relations at Birzeit University, a Palestinian institution, and press secretary for Hanan Ashrawi, the Palestinian Delegate to the Middle East peace process. We visited his home in Jerusalem's Old City, and from the roof of his building he pointed out the major sights, including the Dome of the Rock on the Temple Mount, the oldest Islamic building in the world. From that elevated vantage point, we could appreciate why the city is called "Jerusalem of Gold."

Near the end of 2009, I received an invitation to a "Holiday Celebration" at the White House. It was on vellum paper, not red and green but blue, like the flag of Israel. I guessed that the party was for the Jewish holiday of Hanukkah, and I accepted before somebody discovered they had made a mistake and invited the wrong Steinfield.

It was a wonderful event. The rooms of the East Wing—the Red Room, the library, the Green Room, the East Room—all were decorated for the holidays, including several Christmas trees, Hanukkah notwithstanding. There was ample food, including platters of the traditional potato *latkes* (pancakes), liquid refreshment of all kinds, and a lot of important-looking people.

We gathered in a large room. The president came down a staircase and said a few words. The family of a Jewish Naval officer serving in

Ambassador Maen Rashid Areikat and his wife, Jumana,
at the White House, December 16, 2009

Iraq lit a 1783 menorah, on loan from the Jewish Museum in Prague.
The president and the first lady walked along the rope line and greeted
many of us.

I had a plane to catch, but there was still time for more food and a
few hellos. Eating standing up has never been one of my strengths, so I
asked a man and woman if I could sit at their table.

"Of course," they said, and we introduced ourselves.

"Have you traveled to get here today?" I inquired.

"No, we live here," said the man, speaking with a foreign accent.

"How long?" I asked.

"Six months," he replied.

"Where are you from?"

"Jericho," he answered.

Those of you who paid more attention than I did in Sunday school
will remember that according to the Bible, Jericho is where Joshua led

the Israelites upon their return from bondage in Egypt. Today it is part of the Palestinian Territories, on the West Bank.

"What brings you to Washington?" I asked.

"A new job," he answered. "I am the PLO Representative to the United States." I paused and then mouthed the letters "P" "L" "O", as in "Palestinian Liberation Organization."

We talked some more. His wife is from a small village on the West Bank, they have three sons, and, yes, they know Albert Agazarian very well. After discussing the Middle East peace process and the challenges of leadership in that part of the world, I told them, reluctantly, that I had to leave for the airport.

"Please come and see us," they said. I promised that I would.

"Salaam alaikum" (Arabic for "Peace be to you"), he said.

"Aleichem shalom" (Hebrew for "Upon you be peace"), I replied.

My Russian Visa and the Announcement at Baggage Claim

We decided to go back to Russia in the fall of 2011. This time I made sure that the university's invitation was correct, checked out the visa process on the Russian Consulate's website, and sent the invitation off to New York along with application form, passport, bank check, and pre-paid FedEx return envelope. Just as I had done three years earlier.

A month passed with no response, and the time for our departure was approaching. I then looked more closely at the visa instructions online and saw something I missed the first time. *They no longer accept applications in the mail!*

After kicking myself for such carelessness, I wondered why they hadn't simply opened up my package, seen the mistake, and sent it back to me. So I called the telephone number the Consulate lists on its website. First I got a busy signal, and then no answer. I kept trying, and they kept not answering. I have no idea why they publish a phone number, because it turns out you can't call the Russian Consulate in New York.

So, here it was September, the Russian Consulate had custody of my passport, I wasn't even close to having a visa, and panic was setting in. We had promised to be in St. Petersburg on a certain date, me to teach and the Pianist to perform, not to mention that we had paid for airplane tickets. I somehow managed to find the Consulate's email address, and I sent them a polite inquiry.

The response reminded me of the coatroom woman in Vienna. "You should have come to us in person," they wrote. "Have a good day."

I now understood that they weren't going to send me a visa, so I sent another email, apologized for my error, and asked them to please return my documents, especially my passport. They wouldn't answer the phone, but they wasted no time answering emails.

"dear sir, we can not mail it back cause we do not mail documents back according to our policy."

With that helpful response in hand, I did what I should have done in the first place—I contacted an agency in New York that obtains visas for people. By now it was late, and I fell into the "added charge" category. In order to get a visa you need a passport, which I no longer had. So I made an appointment at the passport office in Boston, and when I arrived I got in line along with a lot of other people who needed a passport in a hurry. That costs extra too.

I then sent off the new passport and the other documents, this time to the agency, and a few days before our departure the visa arrived. Now it was time to pack, and I got out my one-of-a-kind, unique, very large blue suitcase. We flew off to Russia, and they let us in.

We returned to Boston seventeen days later and went directly to baggage claim, where I heard the recorded announcement, "Luggage often looks alike. Be sure to check your bags." No one else has a suitcase like mine, I told myself, groggy from jet lag and looking forward to home, drinkable tap water, and a comfortable bed.

We picked up my big blue suitcase and two smaller pieces, cleared customs, and made our way to the taxi stand. Unfortunately, there was a line, so we had to wait our turn.

A few minutes later, just as we reached the front of the line, my cell phone vibrated. Unlike the Russian Consulate, I *do* answer the phone. "Mr. Steinfield?" a man asked.

"Yes," I answered.

"I'm at baggage claim with your large blue suitcase," he said, "and you must have mine."

And I did. It was almost Thanksgiving, and I felt thankful for luggage name tags and cell phones.

My Icelandic Connection and a Run of Bad Luck

We have a teenage granddaughter named Iris. She was born here but lives in Iceland, her mother's country, making her an "Icelandic-American."

August is a good time to be in Iceland, especially if you like daylight, which is available just about round the clock. Of course, they make up for it in winter. The extra daylight means you can cover a lot in a summer day, and there's a lot to see—volcanic landscapes, glaciers, waterfalls, and hot springs, just to name a few choice sights. And, despite the country's name, the temperature isn't bad, usually around 14 or 15 degrees Celsius. That would be in the 50s or low 60s.

During our first visit, nearly twenty years ago, we went to the Blue Lagoon, a geothermal spa that's good for your skin. The rules there are very strict. You have to shower before you go in and after you come out, no exceptions. There's no rule against leaving your bathing suit behind, however, and that's what I did.

Iceland had a good run for a long time, pretty much from AD 874, when the Norwegians arrived, to 2008. You can read about the early days in the sagas, literature treasured by Icelandics. The country does have a few peculiar traditions, such as a belief in elves, also known as "hidden people." Not *everyone* believes in them, but enough do to prevent building roads in certain places for fear of disturbing their rocky homes.

By the beginning of this century, Iceland was more prosperous than most countries. According to the United Nations, it was the most highly developed country in the world, and the fourth most productive country per capita. Of course, the "capita" is pretty low—320,000 people, excluding elves—less than one-fourth the size of New Hampshire.

Then, in 2008, the economic roof fell in. The banking system failed, the country entered into a deep recession, the krona (that's their currency) fell, and inflation ran into double digits. England and the Netherlands inquired as to just how Iceland intended to pay over $5 billion in debt.

No final word on that yet, but some political leaders have fallen by the wayside, as usually happens in a country when things go wrong.

Then, along came Eyjafjallajokull, the unpronounceable (try "AY-yah-fyah-lah-YOH-kuul") volcano that turned day into night out of season and made most of Europe a no-fly zone for nearly two months. Some countries just can't catch a break.

But some politicians can. Icelanders recently elected Jon Gnarr as mayor of Reykjavik. He's a high school dropout and professional comedian known for a routine where he makes crank calls to the White House, the CIA, the FBI, and New York police stations asking if they've found his lost wallet. A man after my own heart, as those of you who recall my essay about my missing wallet can appreciate. It's easy to understand how he got elected. He promised free towels at public swimming places, including the Blue Lagoon.

Speaking of which, I still have the bathing suit I left behind. We called the Blue Lagoon, they sent it the next day, and I picked it up at the Reykjavik bus station. And the economic news isn't all bad: Iris got a summer job waiting tables.

My Caribbean Cruise and Arriving Late for New Year's

My parents were friendly with the Smiths, who lived on Ridge Avenue with a perfect view of Mt. Ascutney across the Connecticut River. My grandfather always said, "Jane Smith is tops in Claremont."

Mr. Smith's name was Ernest, but no one ever referred to him by that name. He ran the local bottling plant and was known to all as "Coca-Cola Smith." I was friendly with their younger son, Bill, who was a year ahead of me at Stevens High School.

The Smith family decided to take a holiday cruise to the Caribbean, and they wanted someone to come along and keep their son company. They asked my parents if I could go, my mother said yes, and so I got lucky. My girlfriend wasn't thrilled that I was leaving town for the Christmas holidays, but she wasn't all that upset either, and we made plans to spend New Year's Eve together. This was to be a seven-day cruise, and we would be back in town on December 31st.

We embarked from New York Harbor on the Greek Line's *Olympia*. The food on board was wonderful, we sat at the Captain's Table one night, and they had great entertainers on board. We went ashore in Nassau and drank beer at "Dirty Dick's."

In Havana, I smoked my first and last Cuban cigar. That was before Castro, so there was nothing unusual about Americans visiting what was then a pretty wide-open place. Bill and I wanted to go to the famous Tropicana nightclub, but his parents had some concerns about our impressionable young eyes, and the minimum charge was $5 a person, so we didn't go.

I thought about that trip when I read about the unhappy Carnival *Splendor* cruise. Thirty-five hundred passengers, and over a thousand crew members, were stranded at sea, two hundred miles south of San Diego. Three days without electricity, flushable toilets, and other conveniences, and not even a chlorine pump for the on-board pools.

From what I could tell, the passengers were remarkably good-natured about the experience, although they hadn't exactly signed up for toaster pastries, pickle sandwiches, and warm yogurt. Maybe some of the older

Bill Smith and me, Havana, Cuba, 1955

ones remembered the *Andrea Doria* disaster half a century ago, and no doubt many of them had seen the movie *Titanic*.

Still, the voyage was not as advertised. One eight-year-old boy, apparently an experienced traveler, expressed his chagrin at losing room service. "I always get brownies," he told a newspaper reporter. Even worse, according to his mother, there was no cell phone service.

My teenage cruise also ran into a problem, although nothing comparable to the not-so-splendid *Splendor* debacle. As we were entering New York Harbor at the end of our trip, the fog rolled in, and the captain announced that we would be unable to land. Our seven-day cruise turned into eight days, with no shortage of food or electricity. Back then no one worried about cell phones; they hadn't been invented. I'm not sure if I could have given my girlfriend a call from the ship. Probably not.

We disembarked the next day and made our way back to Claremont. I got to my girlfriend's house the evening of January 1st, twenty-four hours late. She greeted me with those memorable words, "Where were you?"

My Left-Behind Snore Guard and Beating a Bum Rap

If you're a man over forty (I am), chances are that you snore (I do). That unpleasant condition afflicts about sixty percent of males, but there is something you can do about it. Wear a snore guard, a small plastic device that opens up the airways. I've been doing so for several years with pretty good results, and I take it with me whenever I leave home. I only own one, so I have my regular routine to be sure I don't forget it when I travel.

Another problem that affects aging males is absentmindedness, and I seem to have that too. I usually remember to bring the snore-stopping device from Boston to Jaffrey. The problem is at the other end, remembering to take it back to the city. If I forget, this not only disturbs my sleep but it also irritates the Pianist.

A year or so ago, I found myself back in Boston with my snore guard still in Jaffrey. The next morning, I decided to take a detour on my way to the office and retrieve the device.

I took the usual route, through Cambridge, part way around Fresh Pond Circle, and onto Route 2 heading west. It was a clear day, not much traffic, and I had the company of a recorded book. About midway into the ninety-minute ride, I saw a blue car marked "State Police" going around fifty-five or so. Taking no chances, I pulled behind the cruiser, which started to slow down—fifty, forty-five, forty. I finally decided to pass.

No sooner did I get back into the right-hand lane than the blue light started flashing. It doesn't take three guesses to figure out what that means. I pulled over and stopped.

The officer sauntered over, slowly the way they do, and I rolled down my window.

No "Good morning" or other niceties, just "License and registration."

I handed over the documents, and he walked back to his vehicle, no doubt to check and see if I was wanted on charges. He returned, finally, handed the papers back to me, and started to write on his pad.

"You were exceeding the speed limit," he said. "I clocked you at seventy."

He handed me a citation, and I resumed my trip to retrieve the snore guard. *This is going to be an expensive night's sleep,* I thought to myself.

A while later, I got a notice in the mail telling me I could pay the fine of $150 or request a hearing. I put the paper aside to think about it. I wasn't sure whether I was or was not exceeding the speed limit, but it couldn't have been by much. So, I decided to contest the ticket.

On the day of the hearing, I showed up at the courthouse on Main Street in a picturesque Massachusetts town. I checked in, took my place on a bench outside the courtroom, and waited for someone to call my name. Within a matter of minutes, I was facing the magistrate, with a police officer sitting at the prosecutor's table. He wasn't the one who had written me up on Route 2, but he had some papers in front of him and read off a version of what had happened. Nothing about the slow-down, let-him-pass, blue-light-that-sucker routine, just that I had exceeded the speed limit.

Then it was my turn. I stood up to speak, and the magistrate said, "You don't have to stand, you can sit."

Without even thinking, I said, "I'm accustomed to standing in court."

"Are you a lawyer?" he asked.

I admitted I was, thinking that would be the kiss of death.

"Case dismissed," he announced.

My Delayed Flight and Taco Bell

Whenever we drive from Boston to Jaffrey, we drive past Taco Bell in Rindge. We're always anxious to get to our house on Gilmore Pond, so we never stop. But each time, I'm reminded of my terrible, awful Florida flight.

It happened several years ago. I was on my way to Puerto Rico on business and scheduled a Florida stopover for a meeting in Fort Lauderdale. *Why not kill two birds with one stone?* I asked myself. And, just to make life easier, I decided to splurge and arrange for one of those drivers you see at the airport holding up a sign with someone else's name on it.

The idea was to fly to Miami, have the driver take me to Fort Lauderdale, check into the hotel, enjoy dinner, and get a good night's sleep. In the morning, I would go to my meeting, get a ride back to the airport, and continue my trip. An excellent plan, I thought.

The plane left Boston late due to bad weather. So, I would eat dinner late, no big deal, actually quite continental. As we approached Miami, however, the pilot told us we were in a holding pattern. That was not good news.

A while later, he announced that the Miami airport was closed and the plane was low on fuel, so we would divert to Tampa, refuel, and by then the Miami airport would have reopened. It sounded sensible as he explained it. We landed in Tampa, refueled, and headed east. By now it was getting close to nine o'clock at night, and there was no food on the plane.

Still, the planeload of passengers remained patient, almost docile. That's how it is when you go by plane. The disembodied captain's voice reassures you, and you believe him.

We landed around ten o'clock. It shouldn't take seven hours to get from Boston to Miami, but these things happen. I still had time to pick up the checked bag, eat, and get some sleep.

Except there was another problem: The captain told us we might be on the runway for as long as forty-five minutes. No gate was available at which we could disembark. An hour later, with no forward motion, not even a pretzel to eat, and nothing to drink, the passengers began getting restless. Flight attendants shrugged, cell phones appeared, and frustration filled the cabin.

By midnight, a revolution was at hand. The flight crew, as upset and overwrought as we were, approved desperate measures: "Sure, call the mayor, call Channel 7, whatever it takes."

At two o'clock in the morning, now eleven hours into the trip from hell, we pulled up to the gate and got off the plane. Half crazed, famished, and bleary eyed, I stumbled towards Baggage Claim. As I approached Carousel 4, there he was, a man holding a sign with *my* name on it. I had completely forgotten about the driver, but he remembered me. Lawyers aren't the only ones who charge by the hour.

So, the worst was over, except that it wasn't. The baggage handlers had given up and gone home, and Carousel 4 was at a standstill, literally.

We stood there, me dumbstruck and the driver doubling as my therapist. "You're fine," he assured me, "and your bag will be here any minute."

Two hours later, and still without my suitcase, I decided that unless I ate something I would die at Baggage Claim. The airport's one open restaurant, Burger King, had a line that stretched as far as I could see, so we made a command decision. We left the terminal, got into the car, and drove off looking for food.

At that hour of the night (or day, by then I wasn't sure), there aren't a lot of open restaurants in the neighborhood around the airport. Then it appeared, like an oasis in the desert—Taco Bell.

Restored by the best meal I ever had, we went back to Miami International, Concourse C. My suitcase came down the chute around seven o'clock in the morning, and off we went to Fort Lauderdale, the car reeking of enchiladas. We got to the hotel an hour later, and the driver said they would send me a bill. I thanked him and went inside.

The desk clerk said, "Good morning, may I help you?"

"Yes," I said, "I'd like to cancel my reservation for last night."

I washed up, went to my meeting, and continued on to Puerto Rico. A few weeks later American Airlines sent me an email apologizing "for any inconvenience we may have caused."

My Atlanta Visit and the Kindness of Strangers

In 1947, Tennessee Williams's play *A Streetcar Named Desire* opened on Broadway. Marlon Brando starred as Stanley Kowalski, and Jessica Tandy played the role of Blanche DuBois. According to *Wikipedia*, Blanche is one of the most recognizable characters in American drama. She preferred "what's magic" over reality, and she drank too much.

When the movie came out in 1951, Brando was still playing the crude and brutish Stanley, but Vivien Leigh had taken over the role of Blanche. The play contains many memorable lines, but the most famous is Blanche's, "I have always depended on the kindness of strangers."

No one ever confused me with Blanche DuBois, and I never aspired to play the role, or that of Stanley for that matter. But I did get to utter that famous line, just once. It happened in Atlanta in 1988.

I was there to attend the Democratic National Convention. My partner, Mike Dukakis, was running for president, and I had agreed to organize a seminar dealing with how to prevent fraud on election day (not to be confused with hanging chads, which came along many years later).

After the session was over, I found myself on the street with two Arizona lawyers—one a young woman, the other an eminent senior lawyer named John Frank, who told me to keep an eye on his young associate who, he said, "is going places."[14] The problem the three of us faced was that we had no way of getting from where we were to our hotel downtown. No car and not a taxi in sight. We couldn't find a pay phone, and I didn't have a clue what to do. Mr. Frank took the matter in hand and waved down a passing motorist. He explained to the driver that we were from out of town, didn't really know quite where we were, and would appreciate a ride to our hotel if it wasn't too far out of his way.

"Hop in," said the driver. "I'll be glad to take you." I think that is what is known as southern hospitality.

---

14   He was right. The young lawyer was Janet Napolitano, who became governor of Arizona and more recently served as Secretary of Homeland Security.

On our way, he pointed out some of the local sights, and then he asked if he could drop us off a block or two from the hotel. "One way streets," he explained. Being a resident of Boston, I understood that problem.

He pulled alongside the curb, and we got out. There, on the sidewalk, was a vendor selling hot dogs and soda under a sign that said "Streetcart Named Devour." I took one look and knew my Blanche moment had arrived.

I turned back to the driver, looked him in the eye, and said, in my best southern accent, "Why thank you, sir. I have always depended on the kindness of strangers."

My Trip to Rosebud and Languages That Won't Die

Yiddish was the language of my ancestors. Many years ago I decided I should learn it, so I took an adult education course. All I remember is *Khop nisht di lokshn far di fish,* which means "Don't grab the noodles before the fish." In English we would say, "Don't put the cart before the horse."

I should have paid closer attention in the class, or listened more carefully to my grandparents when I was young. When they came to this country from the Pale of Settlement, the area in Russia where Jews were allowed to live in the nineteenth century, they brought their language with them. They learned English, but their generation held tight to the *mame-loshn,* the mother tongue.

Language connects us to our past. I was reminded of this recently when I read the obituary of Albert White Hat. Mr. White Hat, a member of the Rosebud Sioux tribe, taught Lakota Studies at Sinte Gliska University on the Rosebud Indian Reservation. The article described how he "helped preserve Lakota language," and went on to say that he was "known across the powwow circuit for his dedication to the Lakota language and culture." He even translated the movie *Dances with Wolves* into Lakota.

I paused over the article because a few years ago I was part of a small group that spent a day on the Rosebud Reservation in Mission, South Dakota. During our visit we saw first-hand that life on the Reservation is extremely difficult, with high unemployment, crime, alcoholism, domestic abuse—all the plagues of society except more so. Yet our hosts could not have been more gracious. We ate traditional Lakota foods at a luncheon, listened to ceremonial Lakota songs and music, and heard the Lakota language. I asked someone to translate the word "Lakota." It means "friend."

As I absorbed this one-of-a kind experience, I thought about how little I knew about American Indians. My education consisted mostly of Saturday afternoons at the Latchis Theatre in Claremont, hearing Tonto say "How" and addressing the Lone Ranger as *kemo sabe* ("faithful friend"). I asked one of the elders whether young people on the reservation spoke Lakota. He answered my question with a weary look and a shrug.

Just a few weeks ago I met Father John Hatcher, S.J., president of the St. Francis Mission Among the Lakota. He was visiting Boston to promote the work of the Mission, which is to address social, spiritual, and educational problems on the Rosebud Reservation. He told me that part of this Jesuit initiative is to help preserve the Lakota language. The Mission's brochure says, "The essential part of a culture is its language; without its language, a culture dies."

Mr. White Hat spent his life keeping a culture alive. The same can be said for his Jewish counterparts who work to preserve the Yiddish language. It may seem odd to couple the two, the cultures of Indians and Jews, but I'm not the first person to do so. In the movie *Blazing Saddles,* Mel Brooks plays a Yiddish-speaking Indian chief who uses such expressions as *zayt nisht meshuge* ("don't be crazy") and *abi gezunt* ("as long as you're healthy"). I grew up hearing those very words.

I know even less Lakota than I do Yiddish, but on my visit to Rosebud I did learn the Lakota word for "hello." Actually, I already knew it from my boyhood days. The word is *hau.*

Claremont

My Sister's Room and Memories of Christmas

My father was born in Chelsea, Massachusetts, in March, 1891. At least he thought that was the month and year. They have fires occasionally in Chelsea, and his birth records went up in one of them.

His father, for whom I am named, was in the junk business, a recycler before that word was invented. He told me that when he was a boy, they used to go by horse and wagon across Massachusetts, and then into New Hampshire. Somehow, they found Claremont and moved there in 1900. The family remained for five generations.

I haven't lived there in a very long time, but I hold clear memories of the Christmas season in the 1940s and '50s. Back then, every storefront window had a store behind it. Festive lights adorned Pleasant Street, and shoppers came from all over Sullivan County.

I wouldn't say that my family was especially observant, but my father grew up with a strong sense of his Jewish identity. After I turned thirteen, he took me to the synagogue every year when he would recite the mourner's *kaddish* on the anniversary of his parents' deaths (known in Yiddish as *yahrzeit*). And he spoke a pretty good Yiddish, which I imagine was the language of his childhood home.

We were one of the fifty or so Jewish families in a town of 12,000. Before we acquired a synagogue and a rabbi in 1948, services were held at the home of Mr. Bloomberg, who was a *shochet* (kosher butcher). I remember learning about Hanukkah, the holiday nobody knows how to spell, and we lit the candles for eight nights.

But in school, of course, it was all Christmas. We sang carols, and if any of the Jewish kids felt uneasy about praising Jesus, we could just mouth the words. Everyone knew we were not celebrating the religious holiday, but no one told us we couldn't enjoy the spirit of the season.

Here, a brief digression. I played junior league basketball and named my team the "Brown Bombers" after my hero, heavyweight champ Joe Louis. I saw the other kids go to the foul line and make the sign of the cross before shooting. It seemed to work for them, so I started doing the same thing. I thought that was how you made foul shots. Eventually,

Phyllis at age 10, 1945

the coach took me aside and explained that particular fact of life to me. So, I stopped crossing myself, which really hadn't done me much good anyway.

Back to Christmas: My sister wanted a tree, and our indulgent father said she could have one, but not in the living room. That was OK, since she happened to have a fireplace in her bedroom. So we had the tree and the lights, stockings, candy canes, and Santa, hidden away upstairs so no one knew.

Eventually, my sister changed her mind, and we stopped having a Christmas tree. I remember thinking it was the right thing to do. It's not our holiday. But I missed it for a long time. Being with my parents and sister, opening our presents—it was special and memorable. Christmas at the Steinfields', second floor, my sister's bedroom.

I'm glad we had those Christmases together. My father died in 1957 . . . on Christmas Day.

My Fifth Grade Teacher and Valentine's Day

In June of 2007, I went back to Claremont for my fiftieth high school reunion. It was a wonderful experience. Everyone who was there wanted to be there, and we still spoke a common language. Some ties really bind.

On Friday night, we gathered at the Moose Hall for dinner and memories. Someone had set up a display of photographs, including class pictures going back to kindergarten. My fifth grade class was included. We didn't just graduate high school in the same year; we grew up together.

I went to the Way School for the first six grades. I remember all my teachers, but every now and then you meet someone special. My fifth grade teacher, Miss Manley, was such a person.

She wore rimless glasses and prim suits, and her dark hair was wrapped in a bun, the essence of neatness. Her look was severe, as was her voice, but she knew how to teach.

She often quoted her "Aunt Minnie" in order to make a point. It took a while for most of us to catch on, but that was the year of *Harvey*, the movie about Jimmy Stewart's tall rabbit friend of the same name, and we finally got it. There was no such person. Even now, more than sixty years later, I can hear the words, "As my Aunt Minnie used to say," followed by some interesting observation about history or math or civics or whatever was the subject of the moment.

Miss Manley and I liked each other. It was she, I think, who taught me to love reading. And in the following years, as I made my way through grades six to twelve, I saw her pretty often at the Pleasant Sweet Shop downtown, or at the Way School when I would drop in for a visit. She was not just my former teacher. She had become my friend.

I went off to college, left the town, and the years passed. I never forgot Miss Manley, but I did not see her or keep in touch. Then, a few years before the reunion, I happened to be in Claremont on Valentine's Day. I said to the Pianist, "I wonder whatever became of Miss Manley."

"Who?" she asked.

Fifth grade, 1950

I told her, "My fifth grade teacher. She made a real difference to me."
"Is she still alive?" the Pianist asked, and I confessed I had no idea.

But, just on a whim, I drove to the Square and parked in front of where she had lived in the 1950s. I entered the old building, and there was her name on the mailbox—"Josephine Manley."

I walked up one flight and down to her apartment at the end of the hallway. I rang the bell, and in a minute, a woman opened the door. I didn't say a word; I just looked at her. She looked back at me, and her first words were, "Oh, Joe, you're my valentine."

My Claremont Youth and the Things We Didn't Have

My mother taught me not to hit back. She thought that it was more civilized, more dignified somehow, to walk away rather than stand your ground. She taught me many useful things, but that one didn't take.

In Claremont, there were many things we didn't have. Minorities, for example. There was one black family, but that was it, and they moved away. No Asians, no Hispanics, no Native Americans. In other words, we were missing many of the groups that help make America a diverse society.

Even without blacks, we sang a song in school, "You can get good milk from a brown-skinned cow; the color of its skin doesn't matter anyhow . . . ." I'm not making that up.

I guess the fifty or so Jewish families were a minority, although no one made much of it. The prism of hindsight can be selective. Maybe there was anti-Semitism in the town, but with one exception, I didn't know about it. In those days, the 1940s and '50s, Claremont was prosperous, and people seemed to get along. It was, in my memory, a tolerant place.

Another thing we didn't have was homosexuality. At least we didn't know we had it. I thought about this recently as the New Hampshire legislature debated whether to join Vermont and legalize same-sex marriage. Sure, there were a few people "in the closet" back then, although that expression didn't exist at the time, but no one said anything. They worked in the stores, taught in the schools, made their own way, and did no harm.

For that matter, we really didn't have sex of *any* kind. As kids we talked about it, but no one actually did it. Well, hardly anyone. I recall that a girl left town one day for the better part of a year, and then came back.

Drugs existed in those days, but in faraway places like New York City, not our town. There was no shortage of alcohol, of course, and I grew up knowing words like "highball" and "nightcap" and "one for the road." Sounds quaint, but back then it was just being social. Like cigarettes. Most people had them out on the table, so guests could help themselves.

Crime was something else we didn't have. Supposedly, there had once been a murder in Claremont, but no one ever talked about the details, like who was the victim or what became of the murderer. One time there was an open house at the police station jail, and I went inside and they closed the door with a loud clank. Funny, the sounds you remember.

Pollution? Of course we had it. The factories, including my father's mill on the Sugar River, contributed to it, but no one ever talked about it. So in that sense, like the tree that falls in the forest with no one there to hear it, it didn't exist either.

I remember the one exception. It happened in the schoolyard during recess. A kid called me a name, referring to my family's religion. I ignored my mother's teaching and hit him. We wrestled on the ground until the principal came out, broke up the fight, and called our mothers. Mine took me home and said something in the car I'll never forget: "Good for you."

My Automobile Memories and the General Motors Bankruptcy

Growing up in Claremont was all about cars. And Cadillac was king.

We didn't have one, but Ronnie Agel's mother did, and it made him special, not to mention the fact that she looked like a movie star. My Uncle Bill had a gray Oldsmobile, and my mother drove a blue Buick, both very nice cars. For some reason, the cars in our family never changed colors, even though they got traded in every two years. When the new models came out, they actually looked different. One year it was lethal tailfins, another year the wraparound windshield. Once in a while they came up with something practical—seatbelts, for example.

My father was the exception to the two-year car rule. He mostly drove General Motors cars, usually a stick-shift Chevy or something like it. He kept a car for as long as it would run, and he didn't seem to care about being out of style. Maybe it had something to do with growing up poor in the horse-and-buggy era, or maybe it had to do with his driving habits. Nothing serious, mind you, but he had a habit of getting into minor accidents.

We told him he should keep his eyes on the road and not look at his newspaper, that era's version of texting while driving. For some reason he only ran into cars being driven by likeable people. I remember that one time it was "a Jewish guy from Philadelphia."

My friend Mike refused to ride with him. One day, we were going downtown to the movies, and my father offered us a lift. Mike politely declined, but I convinced him that we should accept. We got to the Latchis Theatre without incident, and I said to Mike, "I told you so." We watched my father pull away and plow straight into the car in front of him. I don't remember what movie we saw, but I do remember that Mike never took another ride from my father.

Cars had personalities. Take the Chrysler Imperial, for example. It wasn't a Cadillac, but it cost about the same and suited a certain kind of driver, preferably one smoking a cigar, like Sammy Satzow. His son,

Michael, today runs North Country Smoke House and helps keep alive the spirit of Temple Meyer-David.

There was one other member of the expensive "big three," the Lincoln Continental. People who drove them were usually from out of town.

Then there were the cars that time forgot—the sleek Studebaker, the boxy DeSoto, the square Nash, and the stodgy Packard. My all-time favorite, the Edsel, came along when I was in college. It was gone almost as soon as it got here. My father-in-law had one, unloaded it for next to nothing, and cursed his bad luck when they became collector's items.

Back in 1953, GM's president said, "What's good for General Motors is good for the nation." Little did he know how true those words would become. Today, the federal government is in the car business, so what's good for GM really is good for the country, and for Canada too—they own a piece of the company. The lesson to be learned from all of this? Don't make my father-in-law's mistake. Buy a Pontiac.

My Claremont Optimism and the Bankruptcy of Cities

I've only been to Detroit a few times, most recently on a weekend in 2012. What I saw wasn't pretty—block after block of abandoned stores and homes. Today, bankruptcy.

Back in the 1940s and '50s, when I was growing up in Claremont, the only reason I had to think of the two cities at the same time was that my father went to Detroit on business. The Motor City was thriving, with a population of over two million, including my great-uncle Saul Firestone. My father's company, the Claremont Waste Manufacturing Company, made flock, which was used to line glove compartments and trunks. I remember hearing about sales calls to Studebaker and Kaiser. Back then, those companies' cars were pretty popular, but they were gone by the early 1960s. I don't think the flock was to blame.

At that time Claremont was also thriving, and it even converted from being a town to a city. The mills, my father's included, were operating three shifts a day, the stores welcomed shoppers from all over Sullivan County, and the population was stable at around 12,000 or so.

Claremont's population today is about the same as it was then, maybe a few hundred more, and it looks about the same as it did then. Detroit's population has dropped by more than sixty percent, and its look has changed radically, from a flourishing metropolis to one pockmarked by debris, abandoned buildings, and empty blocks. Like so many mill towns, Claremont has gone through difficult times, but nothing like those of Detroit, which in addition to losing more than half its population has the highest crime rate in the country.

A few Sundays ago I drove from Jaffrey to Claremont to meet my best boyhood friends, Ray and Mike, for dinner at the Common Man restaurant. There are still vacant storefronts on Pleasant Street, but the downtown area looks better than it did a few years ago. Housed in what used to be a textile mill on the Sugar River, the restaurant was busy, a good centerpiece for our home town.

Most Claremonters I've known over the years seem to combine equal parts optimism and pragmatism, as if the members of the community collectively recognize that "we'll never be Portsmouth," and maybe not even Keene, but all in all it's not a bad place to live. If I am a "terminal optimist," as the Pianist claims, maybe it's because of where I'm from. Even the city manager has an upbeat name, Guy Santagate. According to him, "Claremont only moves forward now."

Detroit might want to consider inhaling a breath of Claremont optimism. Things can't get much worse after all. Soon they'll elect a new mayor, and the leading candidate is the county sheriff. His last name also seems to fit the situation. It's Napoleon.[15]

Last month the Red Sox traded shortstop José Iglesias to the Tigers. I felt sorry for this promising young shortstop, leaving Beantown for Motown, but then I checked the standings and felt better for José. Like the Sox, the Tigers are in first place in their division. I'm rooting for Detroit to pull out of the financials doldrums, but I hope they don't beat the Red Sox in the playoffs.

I recently found out that in addition to my father's business trips, there is another connection between the two cities. The 1873 map of Detroit, Michigan, was published by the *Claremont Manufacturing Company* of Claremont, New Hampshire. I looked at the company name and did a double take. Then I saw that the word "Waste" was missing and realized it wasn't my father's flock company.

---

15   The sheriff lost, and Mike Duggan, a write-in candidate, was elected to succeed Dave Bing, who had more success as an all-star NBA basketball player than he did as Detroit's mayor.

My Life as a Salesman and the Radio That Never Arrived

When I was nine or ten, I saw an ad in a comic book. You could send $3.99 to an address in Kearney, Nebraska, and get a portable radio that would fit in the palm of your hand. That sounded good to me, so I told my mother I wanted to buy the radio, and could she please give me the money?

"No," she replied. "You'll have to get a job and earn it."

I reminded her that I was only a little kid and could hardly be expected to earn money.

"Just a minute," she said, and the next thing I knew she announced, "Here's something you can do."

What my mother had found in that day's *Eagle* was a classified ad from "Friendship Studios," a stationary company in Elmira, New York, looking for local sales representatives. I'm not sure they had me in mind, but I wanted that radio, so I sent away for a sample kit.

Within a few days, the samples arrived, and my career as a door-to-door salesman began. I started ringing my mother's friends' doorbells to see if they would like to order engraved stationery, or imprinted napkins, or matchbooks, or greeting cards. With my carbon-papered pad, I could write down the order, leave one copy with my customer, and have a duplicate for myself. Back then, this was considered technology. It didn't take long to earn the necessary $3.99, which I sent off to Nebraska as planned.

Soon I branched out, carrying a larger sample kit and ringing the doorbells of strangers. While waiting for my radio to make its way from Nebraska to Claremont, I continued my sales career, and that fall I decided to expand and include Christmas cards.

Maybe I was born to be a door-to-door salesman, because when I needed a summer job after my first year of law school, I spotted a classified ad from the Fuller Brush Company. I remembered the 1940s' movie, *The Fuller Brush Man*, starring Red Skelton, which I had seen at the Latchis Theatre in Claremont, never expecting that I would become such a person.

But history repeats itself, and I did too. Just like old times. I took my sample kit door to door in Boston's North End, this time climbing countless flights of stairs in apartment buildings. I used the same order pads, wrote up the sales, and made deliveries every Friday. Usually, a customer would offer me lunch, almost always pasta, and one frequent question was whether I was Italian.

"No," I would reply.

"What are you?" the customer would ask.

"Jewish," I would answer.

More than once, my customer would say, "Oh, you look Italian. My brother-in-law's Jewish."

I learned valuable lessons that summer. One was the importance of giving advance notice. I had little choice but to let people know I was coming, since that was the summer the Boston Strangler was also cruising the neighborhood. I hired a nine- or ten-year-old kid to drop off brochures, featuring that week's "specials" and letting people know I would be ringing their doorbells. The Strangler didn't do that.

Another lesson was how to "close" a sale. I would demonstrate my most popular product, DCW ("dusts, cleans, waxes"). The North End never had so many shiny coffee tables. Then I would repeat what my supervisor told us to say. Never ask, "Would you like to order one?" Always ask, "Would you like three, or will two be enough for today?"

I've never regretted my door-to-door experience. It helped me develop independence at a young age, and it taught me when to take "No" for an answer. I'm sorry to report, however, that the portable radio never arrived, and I lost the $3.99.

My Hometown Newspaper and a Life Cut Short

New Hampshire has a long and proud newspaper history. Portsmouth's *Gazette* is the oldest newspaper in the country. It has been published continuously since 1756. Keene's *Sentinel* began in 1799, making it fifth in longevity.

My hometown paper, the Claremont *Daily Eagle*, was first published in 1914, although the weekly version goes back to 1834. It became the *Eagle-Times* in the 1970s. The newspaper closed its doors in 2009, joining Albuquerque's *Tribune*, Baltimore's *Examiner*, Cincinnati's *Post*, and the *Rocky Mountain News*, among others. You can find the whole list on a website with the graphic name "newspaperdeathwatch.com." Some groups you'd rather not be part of.

The recent headline, "Hill Family Pulls the Plug," brought back memories from my early years. My father was a newspaper addict, and so am I. Maybe it's a genetic trait.

When I was a kid, we got two newspapers, the *Daily Eagle* and the *Boston Record*. We definitely did not get the *Boston Globe*—too liberal for my conservative father, I suspect—and I don't think I even knew there was such a thing as *The New York Times*. Just to keep the record straight, we didn't get Manchester's *Union Leader* either.

Six days a week, the *Eagle* told us nearly everything we needed to know—who showed up in local court to face Judge Leahy (you didn't want to be in that group either); what was playing at the movies; who was born, got married, or died; what they were serving for lunch at school; and who made the honor roll. I was lucky enough to be in that last group from time to time. I hoped for the day when my name would appear in the sports section as the second baseman for the Stevens High School Cardinals. That day, alas, did not come.

John McLane Clark bought the *Eagle* in 1948. He was tall, handsome, and intelligent. My mother predicted that one day he would follow in his grandfather's footsteps and become New Hampshire's governor. As publisher and editor of the newspaper, he took his time getting to know the town and its people. Despite his patrician private school upbringing and Dartmouth College degree, he became very much a part of our blue-collar town. My parents knew Mr. Clark, and so did I, the way a young child "knows" an adult. My father saw him regularly at Rotary Club luncheons.

A few days before Thanksgiving in 1950, Mr. Clark's life was cut short at the age of thirty-nine. He drowned in an accident while canoeing with three of his children on the swollen Sugar River. He left a wife and five children. The older ones were around my age, and we joined the community in mourning this tragic loss.

Mrs. Clark, the former Rhoda Shaw from Manchester and New Boston, took over the responsibility of raising the children alone, and ownership of the *Eagle* as well. At a time when women rarely did such things, she picked up where her husband left off and became the paper's publisher. The Clarks moved from Broad Street to Edgewood, where they became our next door neighbors. Through good times and bad, Mrs. Clark lived her life with dignity, purpose, and resolve. Like her husband, she helped make Claremont a better place.[16]

---

16 Rhoda Shaw Clark died on August 7, 2011, three weeks short of one hundred years old. By then the *Eagle Times* was back in business, a revival that I'm sure gave her great pleasure. And the McLane family, of which Mrs. Clark was a member by marriage, continues its long history of public service. Annie McLane Kuster now represents New Hampshire as a member of Congress.

My Facts and the Right to be Wrong

"Everyone is entitled to their own opinions,
but they are not entitled to their own facts."

Until recently, I thought that these words came from the late Senator Daniel Patrick Moynihan of New York, and they did, but it looks like he lifted them from someone else.[17] Well, I shouldn't be surprised. As John Adams said, "Facts are stubborn things," even finding out who was the first person to coin a memorable phrase.

Last summer I read an article about facts. According to a study, people who mistakenly believe something don't necessarily change their minds when presented with the facts. Instead, they often become more sure they're right, even though they're wrong.

Here's a good example: A Pakistani scholar who lives near the Afghan border knows for a "fact" that Jewish Americans helped destroy the World Trade Center so that the United States could invade Afghanistan. It wouldn't matter how much information you gave this man. To him, facts are facts, even if they're his facts, and contrary evidence is beside the point.

Here's another: A friend of mine recently told me that unemployed people don't want to work. "It's a fact," he explained.

I suppose that's one of those "facts" that you can't prove one way or the other. I've noticed that oftentimes facts are really just opinions expressed with total certainty. I asked my friend whether he knows any employed person who is eager to become unemployed in order to enjoy the benefits of joblessness. He couldn't think of anyone, so we returned to our usual topic, the Red Sox.

It used to be that yesterday's newspaper wrapped today's fish. Fish consumption keeps going up, but newspaper reading keeps going

---

17 Just who said these words first is uncertain. They have been attributed to the financier Bernard M. Baruch (1870–1965) and to James R. Schlesinger, Secretary of Defense from 1973 to 1975. It was Sen. Moynihan, however, who made them memorable.

down. In the Internet era, something gets published online, you can't use it to wrap anything, and it lasts forever.

How many of you have received emails forwarded by friends or strangers, stating as a "fact" something from the Internet that is completely untrue? I got one stating that eighty-four members of Congress have been stopped for driving drunk, and fourteen have been arrested for drug offenses. I suppose those could be "facts," but they're not—they are completely bogus.

I grew up in an opinionated family on my mother's side. Somehow, they knew what was true. I used to wonder, "How do you know that?" My mother would answer, "That's what people say."

"What people?" I would ask.

Her answer was always the same. "People who know."

As for me, I've got the opposite problem. Maybe I get that from my father. "I love to be wrong," I told my kids when they were young. Since that was often the case, it was a useful way for me to feel.

"Why?" they would ask.

"Because that's how you learn things," I told them. Maybe the recent study that I read about doesn't apply to me.

Or maybe it does. When I was five, my mother and grandmother took me to New York. We went to the Empire State Building, and my mother said, "Joey, that's the tallest building in the world."

"No, it's not," I said. "I've seen a bigger building."

"Where?" asked my mother.

"In Claremont," I told her. And that's a fact.

My High School's Songs and a Gift in Memory

In 1818, the great New Hampshire lawyer and orator, Daniel Webster, argued the *Dartmouth College* case before the United States Supreme Court. He spoke a memorable line, "It is . . . a small college, and yet there are those of us who love it."

I did not attend Dartmouth, and I can't say that I have any particular emotional connection to the school. I did, however, grow up in its shadow. We would drive up from Claremont to eat at the Hanover Inn, attend a football game, or see the ice sculptures at the Winter Carnival.

Once or twice, as a teenager, I managed to crash a Dartmouth fraternity party. What I remember is a lot of beer and pretty girls, mostly blonde, imported from other schools. Dartmouth hadn't even thought of becoming coed back then.

At Stevens High School we had a musical connection to Dartmouth. We took—some might say plagiarized—their songs. This was easy, since both school's names had two syllables. Thus "Glory to Dartmouth" became "Glory to Stevens," "Dartmouth's in Town Again" became "Stevens' in Town Again," and so forth. It was a lot easier than composing your own songs, and cheaper too. In my one year as a high school quarterback, I would hear the band play those songs. In the other years, I would play them myself as a member of the band.

The town of Peterborough planned several events to celebrate its 250th anniversary. One of those was a piano concert, and they invited the Pianist to perform. On the day of the event, she wanted to check out the piano, so we arranged for someone to meet us at the hall where the concert was being held that evening. A pleasant woman awaited us, and she unlocked the door.

After running her fingers up and down the keyboard a few times, the Pianist told me, "This is a great piano."

Acting as if I understood what that meant, I told the lady, who said, "I'm glad to hear it."

This aroused my curiosity. I asked her why, and she said, "I gave it to the town in memory of my husband."

Stevens High School

"What a generous gift," I replied. "Perhaps there's a piece you especially like. The Pianist can play almost anything."

"Well," the woman answered, "my late husband loved music, and he had a particular favorite." Various possibilities ran through my mind—Chopin, Beethoven, or perhaps Brahms.

"Just name it," I told her. You'd think I was the pianist.

Then came the unexpected. "My husband went to Dartmouth," she said, "and he just loved the "Dartmouth Fight Song.""

What choice did I have? "Do you know the "Dartmouth Fight Song?"" I asked the Pianist.

She looked up with a puzzled expression and said, "No, but if you can hum a few bars, I can play it."

She didn't know, of course, about my high school's song-snatching, or even that for a moment or two in my youth I dreamt of being a back who went tearing by. So, I provided the melody and words for the woman's late husband's favorite, "*Dartmouth's in town again, Team! Team! Team!*" The Pianist played it, and the piano's donor smiled.

"My Counselor" and the New Hampshire Impeachment

Starting in 1911, many kids from the Claremont area went to Camp Soangetaha in Goshen, named after a character in Longfellow's "The Song of Hiawatha." The YMCA sold that camp in the 1960s, and since then the local Y camp has been Camp Coniston in Croyden, named after a book written by the other Winston Churchill[18]. Somehow, I like the old name better.

My parents sent me to a camp in Maine, so I never got to Goshen until I arrived as a junior counselor in 1955. The passage of time has clouded many memories, but not all. One was the homemade doughnuts, as good as those Mrs. Murphy used to make in Jaffrey. Another was the orange crates called "ditty boxes." What better place to keep your clothes?

Perhaps most memorable was the honor society, the "Old Guard." Occasionally, in the stillness of a late July night, a call would come from the woods, "The Old Guard is calling," followed by a name. That person would immediately start running towards the voice, there to enter a secret society and receive the highest honor the camp bestowed. In my two summers at Soangetaha, the call did not come for me.

At the end of each camp day, we would lower the flag and sing the camp song, followed by the playing of Taps. *"Day is done, gone the sun . . . ."* Dwight Eisenhower was President, Sherman Adams was at his side, and the world was at peace. If anyone was worried about the future, I didn't know about it. *"All is well, safely rest . . . ."*

In 2000, I served as counsel to the New Hampshire House of Representatives. After conducting an investigation of certain members of the New Hampshire Supreme Court, I became the prosecutor in the impeachment trial of the state's Chief Justice. During August, between the investigation and the trial, we had time to be in Jaffrey. One evening, we were eating at a Peterborough restaurant when a middle-aged man came over and said, "Joe, my counselor!"

I looked up at this stranger and asked, "Who are you?"

---

18 Winston Churchill, American novelist, 1871-1947, lived in Cornish, New Hampshire.

Camp Soangetaha, Goshen, NH 1955

He replied, "I'm John Teague, your camper."

I remembered the name. "From Newport?" (one town over from Claremont) I asked. He nodded.

"But John, that was forty-five years ago."

"Yes," he replied, "I saw you on television. I didn't remember your name, but when I saw your face I said to my wife, 'That's Joe, my counselor.'"

Opportunities like this don't come along every day. I stood up and said, "John, should we do it."

"Absolutely," he answered, and with no further words between us, we sang to the crowded room:

> *Camp Soangetaha, good night to you,*
> *You are the best camp we ever knew*
> *We will be always loyal and true,*
> *Good night, good night to you.*

My Favorite Lawyer and Homeschooled Children

I've noticed that quite a few New Hampshire mothers homeschool their children. Maybe fathers do too, but I haven't met any.

For six months beginning in April of 2000, I represented the New Hampshire legislature in what has become known as the Supreme Court "Impeachment Case." It was my privilege to be part of something so important for the state where I was born and raised. The job came with perks. I had a reserved parking space in the capitol building, an office, and my very own fax machine.

I stayed many nights at the Holiday Inn, ate lunch at the State House cafeteria, and found out where you could get a late night meal in Concord. I met interesting people, including former judges, former wives of former judges, disgruntled litigants, legislators, and reporters.

And I met citizens, including a woman who was homeschooling her children. Late one afternoon, she came up to me in the corridor outside the hearing room where the trial was being held.

"I'm homeschooling my three children," she told me. "I brought them here today to see how our government works. Would you be willing to speak with them?"

"Of course," I said. First I spoke with the two girls, and then with their older brother, a boy of fourteen.

He shook my hand and said. "I've been watching you on television, and you're my favorite lawyer."

"You've made my day," I told him.

A few days later, it came time for closing arguments. I spoke for two hours, reserving one hour for rebuttal. Counsel for the Chief Justice then spoke for three hours. As is typical for lawyers, neither of us had enough time.

Every good closing has a theme, and my opponent's was, "I don't think so." He went through every argument I had made for our side of the case, paused, and then said those words. It was a virtual mantra, repeated over and over to the point where you could see twenty-two New Hampshire state senators practically mouthing the words for him.

I squirmed each time I heard them.

As his three hours wound down, he told about meeting a mother and her homeschooled children a few days earlier. It sounded familiar. He ended his remarks with a rhetorical flourish, asking the senators to send a message to those children that democracy works in New Hampshire. He sat down, and I got up.

I thought for a moment, and then I told of my meeting with the same family, and the son's supreme compliment—"You're my favorite lawyer." That got a laugh.

Not to be outdone, and even though his time had expired, my adversary jumped up and said, "The older daughter said the same thing to me!" That got a laugh too.

I looked at him, then at the senators, then back at him, and resumed my rebuttal with these four words.

"I don't think so."[19]

---

19   A majority of the New Hampshire Senate, sitting as the impeachment "court" in accordance with the New Hampshire Constitution, voted not to convict the Chief Justice. One of the state senators was George Disnard, Claremont's former Superintendent of Schools. Some people believed that the entire proceeding was "payback for Claremont," referring to a series of opinions—the *Claremont* case— written by the Chief Justice. The case deals with the right of New Hampshire children to equal educational opportunities. The irony of my being from Claremont did not escape notice. The impeachment case is the subject of a book by Mary E. Brown, a member of the state senate, entitled *The Impeachment Trial* (Pittsfield, N.H.: Lynxfield Publishing, 2001).

My High School Band and a Lesson in Politics

My father knew Sherman Adams, governor of New Hampshire from 1949 to 1953. Every Christmas, we got a card signed "Sherm and Rachel."

In January of 1957, the Stevens High School Band boarded the train bound for Washington. This was no mere field trip. We were marching in the inaugural parade, thanks to countless rummage and bake sales, car washes, and other community activities that raised over $8,000. It seemed like the whole town came to Claremont Junction to see us off and, four days later, to welcome us home at 2:30 in the morning. "Band Arrives in Soaking Rain," proclaimed the *Daily Eagle*.

After serving as governor, Sherman Adams became President Eisenhower's Chief of Staff, a position he held until the famous vicuña coat episode in 1958. My father told me that if I saw Mr. Adams in Washington, I should introduce myself and send his regards.

Marching down Pennsylvania Avenue that January 21st Monday as part of an inaugural celebration was a uniquely American experience, a keepsake for the collective memory bank of one hundred patriotic young Claremonters.

Stevens let everyone out of school early to watch us on television. The pre-cable era reception wasn't very good, and we later learned that a Cold War army missile mostly blocked us from the camera's view. I was oblivious to that as I marched along, playing my clarinet with Senator Norris Cotton keeping in step right beside me. Governor Dwinell waved to us from the New Hampshire "Live Free or Die" float, just ahead. No sign of Sherman Adams, however.

We attended the inaugural ball that evening and saw the best entertainers of that era, including Pat Boone, Pearl Bailey, and Abbott & Costello ("Who's on First?"). We toured the city, saw the Tomb of the Unknown Soldier, as it was then known, and visited Mount Vernon. On our last day, we went to the Capitol Building.

And there he was, Sherman Adams, standing in the Rotunda. I went straight over to introduce myself.

"Hello, Mr. Adams," I said. "My father sends you his regards."

Senator Styles Bridges

"How nice to see you," he said. "Who is your father?"

I told him. "Frank Steinfield."

"How is your dear father?"

"He's fine, Mr. Adams," I replied.

"And your mother?"

"Also fine," I said.

"Please send them my very best regards," he said. I promised I would, and I took his picture.

Later that day, as the train left Union Station, I told my friends about the encounter.

"I didn't see Sherman Adams," said my friend Mike.

"Well, I did," I said, "and he was very friendly and sent his best wishes to my parents. Look, there's his picture in the newspaper."

Mike handed me the paper and told me to look at the caption, which identified the picture as that of "Sen. Styles Bridges of New Hampshire."

I blanched. "They've got the wrong name."

"No," said Mike, "you've got the wrong Sherman Adams."

When I got home I told the story to my father, who informed me he had never met Styles Bridges.

United States Senate

COMMITTEE ON
INTERSTATE AND FOREIGN COMMERCE

January 31, 1957

Mrs. Frank Steinfield
Edgewood
Claremont, New Hampshire

Dear Irene:

Thank you for your letter of January 29th. It was kind

of you to take the time to write it.

We enjoyed having the Stevens High School Band with us

and were very proud of their appearance.

Ruth joins me in sending regards to you and Frank.

Sincerely,

Norris Cotton
U. S. Senator

NC:eb

I was especially glad to see your son and appreciate his making himself known to me.

N. C.

Letter from Senator Norris Cotton

My High School Newsletter and Carrying the Torch

Some people eagerly await the publication of the *Farmer's Almanac*. Others count the days 'til the mailman delivers the Burpee's Seed Catalog. As for me, it's the Stevens High School Alumni Association *Newsletter*, which comes every spring and proudly reminds us, right under the title, that ours is "The Oldest *Active* High School Alumni Association in the Country."

A few years ago, the 2010 newsletter arrived announcing that "Alumni Day" would be on June 12th. For those who attended Stevens High School, Alumni Day isn't just any day. Pleasant Street in Claremont is adorned with banners proclaiming, "Welcome Back SHS Alumni."

On Friday night of that weekend, the "special" alumni classes, meaning at least the twenty-fifth and fiftieth and maybe others, gather to eat, drink, and reminisce. When I went back for my fiftieth, we convened at the Moose Hall wearing name cards with photos from our Class of '57 yearbook. It took a while, but as the evening wore on, people started to look like themselves.

Saturday is the big day. The parade starts early and goes on forever—bands, Shriners, antique cars, fire engines, Little Leaguers, and floats from every five-year class. The whole town comes out to watch. And, if you're on your class float, you get to watch the people watching you.

Then it's lunchtime. The Pleasant Sweet Shop, where my grandfather held his "office hours" at the counter while drinking coffee, is long gone, but there are some good choices, including the Common Man restaurant located in one of the restored Monadnock Mill buildings on Water Street. The restaurants have competition, however. The "Ladies of the Moose" offer a $4.00 lunch at the high school cafeteria.

The local restaurants won't be so busy that evening, however. The *Newsletter* reminds us of the "Unspoken Rule"—no competing class events between 6:30 and 9:00p.m. That slot is reserved for the alumni banquet at the Frederick W. Carr Gymnasium. They'll serve Yankee Pot Roast.

The *Newsletter* included "Class News" going back to the Class of 1940, who were looking for a "big showing" for their seventieth. The Class of 1942 lamented that its ranks were getting smaller, but if it's sunny on June 12th, many members planned to show up—fair weather alums, it seems. The Class of 1960 was hatching its plans for the "Big One" out of a farmhouse in Ascutney, Vermont. For some reason, there was no report from the Class of 1985, but I had no doubt they'd be there in large numbers for their twenty-fifth.

I loved the column entitled "When Claremont Sleeps" by "Edna Kemp, Class of 1918." I never met Ms. Kemp and wondered about her present whereabouts, but the *Newsletter* was silent on that subject. "Charles B. Fletcher, '56" contributed another update, "Notes from the Past." I remember Charlie.

And, under "Alumni Spotlights," came a report that Tim Foisy, Class of '78 and now residing in Canada, was one of ten Royal Canadian Mint employees chosen last year to help carry the Olympic Torch across Canada to Vancouver. The entire trek took 106 days. Tim, the report continued, had "accepted an invitation from the Alumni Association to participate in our annual parade on June 12th."

No doubt you can now understand my great fondness for the *Newsletter*. It contains information you won't find anywhere else. As for being the oldest "active" alumni association, I've always wondered about the word "active." Is there, somewhere out there, an even older alumni association that is "*inactive*?"

My Senior Year and the Most Important Teacher

Whenever I think about my four years at Stevens High School, I remember the first day of my senior year. The class was College English, the teacher the legendary Mr. Paquette. I sat in the middle row, front seat, whether by choice or assignment I don't recall. We all knew that for this class, and this teacher, you got there on time and sat up straight.

The short, balding, bantamweight teacher entered the classroom, wearing a dapper tweed sports jacket, rep tie, and charcoal gray slacks.

"Good morning," he began, in his precise tone of voice. "This is College English. My name is Normand Paquette. During class, your eyes will be on me at all times. If I walk across the front of the room, your eyes will follow me. Is that clear?"

He could have simply said, "I expect you to pay attention," but somehow the way he put it was more effective. His message was clear beyond doubt: "We're not kidding around here." No one raised a hand seeking clarification.

The next nine months were a remarkable learning experience for this fortunate group of about thirty high school seniors. For Mr. Paquette, teaching wasn't a job, or even just a calling. It was his passion.

I'm embarrassed to say that I appear to have taken my eyes off that man at least once and got caught in the act. The Class of '57 Yearbook picture of Mr. Paquette shows me, right in front of him, looking down at my desk. I like to think that with that unfortunate exception, I followed his opening day orders.

Our class wasn't just about the great writers and poets and playwrights. It was about the written word. Mr. Paquette taught us how to read and how to write. He made us diagram sentences. Nouns, verbs, objects, prepositions, adjectives, adverbs, punctuation marks—all suddenly took on new meaning. In a sense, he taught us how to think.

And there were rules to be followed. To this day I hate split infinitives. It just isn't right to completely overlook such things.

The educational standing of the United States has slipped terribly since I was a high school senior. We rank seventeenth, behind Finland,

Normand Paquette

South Korea, Japan, and Singapore, among others. Finland provides it students with the best public education in the world. In that country, teaching is considered a high-status profession, and teachers are well paid.[20]

Mr. Paquette was French Canadian, not Finnish, and I'm sure he was paid far less than he was worth. But he never questioned the value of what he did. When he retired, more than twenty years after our graduation, he said, "I've never been sorry I came to Stevens. I've had a very fortunate life."

As for me, I've been blessed with many good teachers, beginning as early as Miss Manley, my fifth grade teacher at the Way School, and extending beyond Stevens High to Brown University and Harvard Law School. But when I measure my teachers by their impact, it's no contest. I don't know whether Mr. Paquette was the best teacher I ever had, but he was the most important.

---

20   The Organization for Economic Cooperation and Development recently reported that in 2012 the United States ranked 22nd in math test scores for 15-year-olds. Shanghai, China, was first. See "Why Other Countries Teach Better," New York *Times*, December 18, 2013, page A22.

My College Applications and the Dreaded Thin Envelope

Nowadays, college admissions offices notify applicants whenever they feel like it, mostly in March. Many of them send emails instead of letters. What this means is that high school seniors can find out on their laptops or smart phones where they will or will not be spending the next four years.

It used to be that colleges sent these notices by regular mail for delivery on April 15th. Back then, of course, there was no such thing as email. Applicants hoped for thick envelopes containing an acceptance letter together with forms to fill out and return. The dreaded thin envelope meant no enclosed forms and you weren't going to that school.

Every April, I think back to my college application experience. I applied to three colleges, but two of them didn't really count as far as I was concerned. I was going to Yale because the Leahy brothers from Claremont had gone there, and I wanted to be like them. I'd also heard it was a good college.

Along with many of my Stevens High School Class of '57 classmates, I awaited the arrival of April 15th. Things didn't go exactly according to plan. In mid-March, my third-choice school, apparently trying to get ahead of the competition, mailed out its notices. Mine arrived in a very thin envelope. Rejected!

I went to see the principal, "Doc" Lord, who told me not to worry. "You'll get into Yale," he said confidently, "and that's where you want to go anyway."

"That's true," I replied, "but I'm not off to a very good start. I've been turned down by my 'safety' school, and I'm not feeling very safe."

He offered to make a phone call to see why that particular college hadn't seen fit to take me. The next day, he told me he had spoken to the admissions officer, who said they had given my application careful attention but decided their school wasn't my first choice, and they preferred to admit students who wanted to go *there*, meaning not Yale.

"He did say they would take another look at your application," "Doc"

Lord told me. "But don't worry," he added. "You'll be going to Yale."

Around the end of March, the school that had rejected me, the one that wasn't either my first or my second choice, sent me another thin envelope.

It's too thin to be an acceptance, I thought to myself. *They can't reject me twice, can they?*

I discovered that there is a third possibility. The letter said, "We have reconsidered your application and congratulations, you're on the waiting list."

I didn't give that particular school any further thought. I was going to Yale, after all. It was really just a formality, waiting for confirmation on April 15th.

That date fell on a school day, and when I got home for lunch there were two thin envelopes on the front hall table, one from school number two and one from Yale. Both letters said the same thing—you're not accepted and you're not rejected.

So there I was on three waiting lists, with no place to go. I waited some more, seventy-three days to be exact.

On June 27, 1957, my sister and I were preparing to leave for upstate New York, where we both had jobs at a summer camp. We packed her car after breakfast, and then I said, "Let's wait until the mail comes." She didn't have to ask why, and neither did my parents.

We waited a couple of hours for the mailman to appear. He handed me one thick envelope and two thin ones. School number three, the one that had both rejected and waitlisted me in March, was the thick one. College number two said no, and so did Yale.

So much for "Doc" Lord's assurances and following in the footsteps of the Leahy brothers. "I'm going to Brown," I announced, and off we drove.[21]

---

21 A few weeks after this piece was published, *The New York Times* published a front page article, "On a College Waiting List? Sending Cookies Isn't Going to Help." (*New York Times,* May 12, 2013). According to the article, the surgeon father of a waitlisted student offered the Dean of Admissions at Union College her choice of free rotator cuff or carpal tunnel surgery, neither of which she needed. I don't think it ever occurred to my father to offer Yale a free truckload of flock. That wasn't his way.

My Latest Reunion and Where to Stay Next Time

I loved every minute of my fiftieth high school reunion. We had excellent accommodations at the Goddard Mansion Bed & Breakfast, not far from my boyhood home at Edgewood. I've written about the annual Stevens High School Alumni Association *Newsletter*, which "contains information you won't find anywhere else." This past spring, the reunion newsletter arrived as usual, reminding us to show up on Pleasant Street on June 11 for the big Alumni Day parade, which promised to be bigger and better than ever.

I didn't make it back to Claremont this time, but the parade went off as scheduled despite a downpour. But I did attend my fiftieth college reunion. As the Memorial Day reunion weekend approached, I had mixed feelings. Would I recognize people? Would they recognize me? Would we find things to talk about? I considered dropping out at the last minute.

But I didn't. So off I went, arriving in Providence along with classmates from near and far. The owner of New Hampshire's minor league baseball team, the Fisher Cats, came from his house, right next to the campus, while another member of the class came from Australia. As I registered, two classmates came over, and we recognized each other immediately. Funny how we haven't changed.

Twenty-five years ago, our college class was headquartered in a dormitory called Arnold House. I would not have remembered that except for a "time capsule" in which we placed notes to be opened twenty-five years later. I wrote, back in 1986, that the Arnold Lounge was "an awful place" and hoped that "maybe we'll do better next time."

No such luck. This time they assigned us to a dormitory, coincidentally called Goddard House, which made me long for the Arnold Lounge. I thought I even recognized some of the trash piled up in plain sight.

To make matters worse, when I filled out the registration form months before, I checked the "yes" box to stay on campus free of charge. So, there I was Friday night, on the second floor in a room hardly fit for human habitation, much less for a member of the "distinguished" fifty-year class. Other than sharing the name "Goddard," it bore no resemblance to our plushy Claremont lodgings four years earlier. I don't know what I expected, but my first thought upon entering that room was, *Serves you right. Next time, don't be such a cheapskate.*

Then I went down to the shared bathroom and discovered there was no hot water. That, combined with an unsleepable mattress and the constant noise outside the window, was all I needed. No Saturday overnight for me. Luckily, I'm in the "near" category, meaning that the decision to drive back to Boston and my own bed (and hot water) was easy to make.

People who attend reunions often think in terms of twenty-five year intervals. Looking ahead, I'm not *hoping* to attend my seventy-fifth Stevens High School reunion, and I'm not *planning* on it, but I'll tell you this—I *intend* to be there. That's known as "optimism."

After my recent college reunion experience, I wrote a letter to the president of the university, telling her about the conditions at Goddard House. She quickly replied that she had looked into it, confirmed that things weren't as they should have been, and promised to make sure they do better in the future. That's good enough for me.

Like Stevens High School, Brown University had a lot to do with shaping my life. It wasn't where I had planned to go, but after turning me down they took me, and it turned out pretty well.[22] If I do make it back for some future reunion, however, there will be one change. Even with the president's assurances, I intend to stay at a hotel.

---

22 My father visited me at Brown, on Parents' Weekend my freshman year, just a few weeks before he died. As we walked on the Old Campus, he said, "You know, I think this turned out to be a good place for you."

My Small World and a Trip to the Past

They say it's a small world.

In 1937, my father bought a house on Lake Sunapee, in the town of Newbury, New Hampshire. During my childhood we spent our summers there, sixteen miles from our house in Claremont. In those summers I learned how to swim, fish, handle a boat, and catch frogs. I used to jump off the boathouse roof into the lake.

My mother sold the house when I was in college, and I never went back. Yet I carry that cottage in my mind to this day—its look, its smell, its sprawling front porch with a chaise lounge, a green glider, and a hammock suspended from the ceiling.

When the time came for me to consider getting a vacation house, back in the 1980s, I didn't consider Lake Sunapee. I preferred to keep my memories the way they were, and, they say, you can't go home again. Or maybe you can.

I was at a conference in Florida a few years ago and ran into an acquaintance named Eve Burton, who lives in New York. She was there with her family, and we struck up a conversation by the pool. I mentioned being from New Hampshire. She asked where, and I told her Claremont. She asked if I knew a woman named Syd Jarvis, and I said that I did. Our families knew each other when I was growing up.

"We go to New Hampshire in the summer," said Eve, "and Syd is like a member of our family."

"Where do you go?" I asked.

"Lake Sunapee," she replied.

"That's a coincidence. We had a place there when I was young."

"Where was it?" Eve asked. I told her it was near the State Park Beach. She nodded. "How did you get there?"

I told her. "It's easy. You just take a right at the traffic circle, drive past the entrance to the beach and up the road for about a mile, and it's on the right."

"Who were your neighbors?" she asked.

I remembered them very well. "The Holmes family."

Phyllis and me

Our "cottage" on the lake

Eve's expression changed. "Was your house before or after the Holmes's house?"

"Right after their house, the very next one," I answered.

Eve paused, smiled, and said, "That's *my* house." Her father bought it in the late 1960s, and she has gone there summers ever since.

The next summer, the Pianist and I spent a day at her Lake Sunapee house with Eve and her family, and Syd Jarvis too. My father would have been pleased. Apart from some tasteful refurbishing, it looked exactly as it did the last time I was there, in the early '60s, which was how it had looked in the late '30s. And it felt the same. When I mentioned this to Eve, she said, "Why change something that's perfect?"

We stepped out on the porch. I looked out across the lake. The beautiful unspoiled greenery on the opposite shore had not changed. Then I saw Eve's young son, running across the boathouse roof towards the water.

I guess they're right. It is a small world.

My House at Edgewood and the Second Lightning Strike

I assumed the coincidence of meeting the woman who now owns the house on Lake Sunapee where I, spent my childhood summers was a one-time thing. They say lightning doesn't strike twice in the same place, but I'm not so sure. This will be, in a sense, a tale twice told.

Except for two months at "the Lake" (which I thought was Lake Sunapee's name when I was young), we lived sixteen miles away. My first address was "26 Francis Street, Claremont." Beginning in 1943, we lived at "Edgewood." Not "Street," not "Circle," not "Drive," simply "Edgewood."

It was really just a long driveway, with a fork that went on the left to two houses and on the right to a third house. Our house was the one on the right, and when my parents bought it they ruined a perfect symmetry: It had been an enclave of the "three Fs"—"the Fosters, the Freemans, and the Frys." We were an "S." I never forgot the name of the people who owned our house before we did. The Frys.

It was a very nice house, with a lot of land that was ideal for the baseball games of my youth, and it even came with a clay tennis court, which was not something my parents really needed. Until he got sick, my father spent most of his time at the mill, or at the Elks Club, and my mother, except for her short stint as a skier, pretty much avoided sports and stuck to the bridge club, the sewing club, and volunteer work.

I lived there until I went off to college, and my mother remained for many years thereafter, living alone in a large house. It may have still been known as "the Fry house," as our house in Jaffrey, after nearly thirty years, is still "the Cann house." It's a New England thing.

Jeff Pyle, a young lawyer with whom I have worked for many years, returned from a memorial service for his grandfather, known as "Toke," who lived his entire adult life in Plymouth, Massachusetts. After the service, Jeff was looking at Toke's "baby book," and he ran across a letter in an envelope with a Claremont return address. Jeff knew I was from Claremont, and the next day he asked me, "Did you ever hear of the Fry family?"

"Why yes," I said, "my parents bought our house from people named Fry."

He then told me what he had learned the day before. Toke's father, Russell T. Fry, Sr. (Jeff's great-grandfather) was the son of Thomas W. Fry of *Edgewood*, Claremont! So, it seems that my friend Jeff's great-great-grandfather, born during the Civil War, owned *our* house. He built it, sometime around the year 1910.

You might even say that lightning struck three times. The letter that Jeff found was dated February 18, 1946. The sender was Mrs. Thomas W. Fry, Jeff's great-great-grandmother. It looks like Edgewood was not the only house that our two families had in common. The return address read, *26 Francis Street*, Claremont, New Hampshire.

Our house - 1943

My First Job and the Question of Identity

An elderly widow in Claremont, Mrs. Newell, owned a large, black Cadillac. She gave up driving, but not the car, meaning that someone at either Stevens High or St. Mary's got to be her after-school chauffeur, and to drive her and her friend Miss Baum to church on Sunday.

When my friend Bob graduated in 1956, he chose me as his successor, which is how I got my first paying job, not counting selling cards and stationary door to door. Mrs. Newell treated her drivers extremely well, paying the unheard-of sum of $1.50 per hour. This was when the going rate for babysitters was 50 cents an hour, 75 cents after midnight.

Mrs. Newell liked taking drives in the countryside, especially during the foliage season, and we would talk as we visited surrounding towns. She was an educated woman, Smith College Class of 1898, with many interests. One time, between Newport and Goshen, we got to talking about religion. I hadn't thought about that conversation in a long time, but it came back to me recently when I read about Cardinal Lustiger's funeral.

Aaron Lustiger was born in 1926, the son of Polish Jews who had emigrated to France after the First World War. In 1939, they moved from Paris to Orléans, and there the young Aaron converted to Catholicism and was baptized as "Aaron Jean-Marie." The Lustiger family survived the war with one exception; his mother was sent to the concentration camp at Auschwitz and died there.

Aaron Jean-Marie became a Catholic priest, worked his way up in the Church, and became Archbishop of Paris in 1981. Two years later he was elevated to Cardinal, a Prince of the Church. Throughout his life, he straddled the circumstances of his birth and his choice of religion and vocation.

"I was born Jewish," he said, "and so I remain. To say I am no longer a Jew is like denying my father and mother, my grandfathers and grandmothers." As might be expected, he came in for criticism from both Jews and Catholics.

He remained steadfast in his belief that he knew who he was and was proud of his identity. Like his parents, he spoke Yiddish, and throughout his life he practiced at least one Jewish ritual. Every year, on the anniversary of his mother's death (the *yahrtzeit*), he went to the synagogue in Paris to recite the *Kaddish*, the Jewish prayer for the dead. At the beginning of his funeral, at Notre Dame Cathedral in 2007, his cousin said the *Kaddish* for him. The prayer is said in Aramaic, the language Jesus spoke.[23]

By now you may be wondering what all this has to do with Claremont and Mrs. Newell. On that autumn day, when the topic of conversation turned to religion, she confided in me, "I haven't known many Jews in my lifetime."

Then she paused and added, "Of course, there's Miss Baum," referring to the close friend whom we picked up and took to the Episcopal Church on Broad Street every Sunday. "She's Jewish."

---

23 The *Kaddish* prayer praises God and contains no reference to death.

My One-Telegram Relatives and a Hero of Argentina

Relatives who couldn't make it to my *bar mitzvah* sent telegrams. I remember just one of them, "Best wishes from Family Samsanowitz." My father told me they were his relatives in Buenos Aires, Argentina. I had never heard of them before, and I've heard nothing of them since. They are my "one-telegram" relatives.

"Family Samsanowitz" fell out of mind until recently, when I read an article about the "Jewish gauchos" of Moisés Ville, Argentina.[24] In the 1940s, there were 5,000 Jews living on that grassland outpost. Like the Jews of Claremont, many of them, or their parents, fled Czarist Russia in the late nineteenth and early twentieth centuries. Today, again like Claremont, their numbers have dwindled, and the last remaining Jewish gauchos have mostly traded in their horses for Ford pickup trucks.

I can't picture any of my relatives galloping in from the pampas, but the article includes a picture of Abel Gerson herding his cows. In the Old Country, the Gersons were named "Gershuni," and my Cousin Janet claimed that all the Gershunis are related. My grandmother's maiden name was Gerson.

In the fall of 1951, a Dartmouth senior from Connecticut decided he wanted to become a rabbi. What better way to start than to attend *Shabbos* (or "*Shabbat*") services on Friday night, and the closest synagogue happened to be Temple Meyer-David in Claremont. At that time, I was preparing for my *bar mitzvah* the following March.

My parents met this young man, and he became a regular Friday dinner guest at our home. He was the sort of person you don't forget, even if you were only twelve when you met him. He was charming, smart, and movie-star handsome. He graduated from Dartmouth, and that was the last I saw of him. I heard he went on to become a rabbi.

The next time I came across his name was in the early 1980s, when I read a book called *Prisoner without a name, Cell without a number,* written by the Argentinian journalist Jacobo Timerman. The book tells

---

24 "Outpost on Pampas, Where Jews Once Found Refuge, Wilts as They Leave," *New York Times,* June 10, 2013, p. A6.

My Bar Mitzvah—Rabbi Maggal (left), Marshall Meyer (right)

about Timerman's imprisonment and torture during a very bad time in Argentina, when thousands of people were "disappeared" under a military dictatorship. When I opened the book, I read the dedication: *"To Marshall Meyer, a rabbi who brought comfort to Jewish, Christian, and atheist prisoners in Argentine jails."*

Marshall Meyer, our Dartmouth College, Friday night dinner guest from thirty years earlier, had become the rabbi of the largest synagogue in Buenos Aires. More than that, when the military took over the country and imprisoned thousands of citizens, he became a human rights hero. Using his considerable personal charm and powers of persuasion, he saved hundreds of lives. After democracy was restored, Argentina awarded him its highest honor, the Order of the Liberator General San Martin.

Bar Mitzvah certificate, 1952

In 1952, he was not even a rabbinical student, much less a rabbi, but my parents asked Marshall to co-preside at my *bar mitzvah*. I can still picture him standing next to me on the *bimah* (the raised platform in the front of the synagogue), and my photograph album from that day shows the young, handsome student looking at me with a thoughtful expression as I raised my hands to God.

So far as I know, no one has written about Marshall Meyer's visits to Claremont. For a brief time, he was one of us. I wonder whether, in later years, he knew my relatives, the Family Samsanowitz.[25]

---

25 Marshall Meyer left Argentina in 1984 and became rabbi of Congregation Bnai Jeshurun in New York, where he served until his death in 1993 at age 63. In 2006, Dartmouth College established an annual human rights lecture in his name.

My Unwritten Book and The Jews of Claremont

Some years ago, I was at a party in Francestown, New Hampshire, and I met a man who had moved from Ohio to New Hampshire. He was Jewish, and when he learned that I was too, and that I had grown up in Claremont, he asked, "What was it like?"

I thought for a minute. "It was wonderful."

We talked some more, and I told him that my father and his family had moved to Claremont in 1900, the second Jewish family in the town. My mother's family moved down from Berlin in 1930. He said, "You should write a book. You could call it *The Jews of Claremont.*

"Good idea," I said, and promptly put the subject out of my mind.

Several months later, the Claremont *Eagle Times* interviewed the Pianist, who was giving a piano recital at the Opera House. When we got to Claremont the following week, and I read the interview, my eyes went straight to the following quote: "My husband is writing a book, *The Jews of Claremont.*"

You can imagine what it was like at intermission, as old friends came up to me and asked, "How's the book coming?"

Of course, it wasn't coming at all. It was then, as it remains today, unwritten.

Yet, over the past few years, I have written pieces of such a book, now collected in these pages. About my grandfather Firestone, who started the Jewish cemetery. About my grandmother, who fed Jascha Heifetz when they still lived in Littleton. About my cousins Martin and Stephen, the refugees who came after the war. About my father, who owned a mill by the Sugar River. About Mr. Gelfand, the tailor who rescued me as a boy when I tore my pants.

I could write about many others. Mr. Bloomfield, the only one I can remember who was actually tall. I think his family were the first Jews of Claremont. After my father died, he stayed with him all night at the funeral home, saying prayers in the Jewish tradition. Mr. Shulins, who ran the dry goods store and spoke an especially "good English." Mrs. Rosenberg, who grew up in Holland and survived a concentration camp. Mr. and Mrs. Brody, who ran a Jewish delicatessen on lower Main Street. Rabbi Michael Szenes, our first rabbi, who survived the war and came from Hungary in 1948.[26] Mr. Jacobson came from South Africa and spoke English with an entirely different accent. These men and women, all immigrants, surrounded my youth.

Today, there are very few Jews living in Claremont. In the 1950s, however, the town's population of about 12,000 included fifty or so Jewish families. I don't know how many people. They always referred to the number of families which, I suppose, tells you something. A small minority, but still a community, of which my family was a part.

We even had a synagogue, Temple Meyer-David, named after Meyer Satzow and David Blumberg, the two Jewish boys from Claremont who died in World War II. Rabbi Szenes's successor, Rabbi Maggal, married a local girl, presided at my *bar mitzvah*, and then went to Hollywood as a consultant to the 1956 Cecil B. DeMille movie *The Ten Commandments*.

Who were the Jews of Claremont, and where did they come from? Many, like my parents, were first-generation Americans. Others, like my grandparents, were immigrants who came from the Old Country early in the twentieth century. They were mostly shopkeepers and tradesmen.

They never lost their accents, or their love for this country. Why did they come to New Hampshire? I remember hearing one explanation.

---

26 Rabbi Szenes left Claremont for Concord in 1952, and then moved in 1959 to Schenectady, New York, where he was the rabbi at Congregation Gates of Heaven until he retired in 1984. No matter where he was, Rabbi Szenes was always our family's rabbi. He came back to Claremont to preside at my father's funeral (1957), my sister's wedding (1958), and our grandparents' funerals (1960 and 1970). He co-presided at my first wedding, in Albany, New York (1961).

When our mother died in 1998, my sister and I called him in Schenectady and asked him to officiate at her funeral in Boston. He was 81, but he accepted immediately. We arranged for a driver, and he came the next day to Levine's Funeral Home in Brookline. We were so grateful and told him he didn't need to add the strenuous drive to Claremont, and then across Vermont to return home. It had already been a long day for him. He wouldn't hear of it. "I need to finish what I've started," he told us. So he officiated at the graveside ceremony at Temple Meyer-David Cemetery as well. It was his last visit to Claremont. He died in 2010 at age 93.

They came for the *luft*, the Yiddish word for air. I don't think that was the only reason.

I once asked my grandfather if he would like to go back and visit his birthplace, Bobrovich in Russia, or maybe it was Poland. He answered with a dismissive wave of the hand and without a moment's pause. "No!"

It wasn't just that he had unhappy memories of a repressive government, and pogroms. It was also that once he set foot on American soil, from Ellis Island to Boston to New Hampshire, he was here to stay. I suspect the others, all from *shtetls* (small villages) in Eastern Europe, felt the same way.

Why did I tell the man from Ohio that growing up in Claremont was "wonderful?" I don't think it was just because the 1950s were a peaceful time, and the world seemed like a safe place. I don't think it was because one always remembers about how good things used to be.

I think it was because growing up in Claremont was a special and secure experience. The Jews of Claremont were part of the community. We were simply Claremonters, and I have identified myself as such ever since.

Book design by Kirsty Anderson
Typeset in Robert Slimbach's Arno Pro
with titles in Michael Harvey's Ellington
Cover design by Henry James
Manufactured by Versa Press